THE WORLD CHESS CHAMPIONSHIP

KORCHNOI vs. KARPOV

by

RAYMOND KEENE

The Inside Story of the Match

SIMON & SCHUSTER
NEW YORK

Library of Congress Cataloging in Publication Data

Keene, Raymond D.
   World chess championship : Korchnoi vs. Karpov.

   1. Chess--Tournaments. 2. Korchnoi, Viktor, 1931—
3. Karpov, Anatolii Evgen'evich, 1951—   I. Title.
GV1455.G388   794.1'57   78-16067
ISBN 0-671-24647-X
ISBN 0-671-24648-8 pbk.

© Raymond Keene 1978
First published in the USA
1978 by Simon & Schuster

Printed in Great Britain

SYMBOLS

+	Check
!	Good move
!!	Excellent move
?	Bad move
??	Losing move

CONTENTS

PART I

PART II

PART III

1

THE UNREAL WORLD— AN INTRODUCTION TO THE WORLD CHAMPIONSHIP 1978

On 18th July in Baguio City in the Philippines the first game was played in the 1978 World Chess Championship.

There has not been a title fight for six years, not, in fact, since the notorious Spassky-Fischer encounter at Reykjavik in 1972, which finally broke the Soviet monopoly dating from 1948. Fischer's case was curious. After becoming World Champion in the most highly publicised chess match of all time, he simply stopped playing, and his three-year reign was marred by total absence of any chess activity on his part. When he also showed no willingness to defend his title after the stipulated three-year period, Anatoly Karpov of the USSR (winner of the 1974 Candidates' tournament) was declared World Champion by default.

To most observers Fischer's conduct was, at best, dereliction of duty to the public and, at worst, insane, yet Fischer's withdrawal was comprehensible in one sense: having once scaled the peak of an intellectual Everest there is a certain psychological reluctance — even a mental block — against performing the feat a second time. Fischer seems to have regarded himself as 'World Champion', and saw no necessity to prove this fact again. Those World Champions of the past who have descended from Olympus to defend their hard-won titles have, by eventually losing to the most worthy challenger, ultimately compromised their reputations, however infinitesimally. By total withdrawal Fischer, like his compatriot Morphy, preserved a mythical nimbus of invincibility. But achievement cannot be allowed to stagnate. If one rests on one's laurels for too long, they wither and perish. The world has passed Fischer by, an isolated figure on his lonely summit, while the centre of attention has shifted inexorably towards those who are actively involved in the struggle — Karpov and Korchnoi.

Anatoly Karpov and Victor Korchnoi could hardly form a greater contrast. Karpov is a model Soviet citizen, a golden boy of the establishment, who, at 27 years of age, has enjoyed an unbroken and brilliant path of success without a single serious setback. Korchnoi, at 47, has reached the top by a more lengthy and arduous method, having qualified for the Candidates' tournament on no less than five occasions, but nearly always faltered at the final hurdle. But what differentiates him most sharply from Karpov is his attitude to the Soviet state. Half Jewish and always prone to rebellious sentiments and contentious statements,

Korchnoi went the whole hog in 1976 and defected from the USSR, alleging that the state was interfering with his professional career. In spite of the upheaval in his personal affairs, Korchnoi's defection was the occasion of a marvellous upsurge in his play, as can be seen from the fact that he won the 1977 Candidates' with relative ease, disposing of three of his former Soviet colleagues (Petrosian, Polugayevsky and Spassky) en route.

There can be no doubt that the match in Baguio is a contest between the two foremost active Grandmasters of the day. The evidence of their respective tournament and match performances is given in chapters 2 and 3, while the most recent Elo calculations for the two put Karpov at 2720 and Korchnoi at 2704. The Elo rating is a statistical method of determining a player's current strength: 2200 on the scale indicates a Master; 2400 plus should represent the International Master level, while at 2500 Grandmaster territory begins. A player who reaches 2600 should be thinking in terms of qualifying for the Candidates' tournament, while 2700 (a rare distinction) reveals a player of World Championship class. The latest figures prove that both Karpov and Korchnoi are within this narrow band, while the third highest rated player, Spassky, is well below at 2648.

These Eleusinian numerals are deeply symbolic. Existence for top chessplayers has a strange, hermetic quality, which ignores common certitudes and practicalities, concentrating instead on the achievement of success in a highly abstract field. Karpov is a slight figure with a high-pitched voice. He only seems to live when he is at the chessboard, and even there the signs of animation are subdued, but in a very quiet way he is enormously self-confident. There is even one theory which suggests that his self-confidence is the product of hypnosis — hence his ability to play so quickly (see chapter 7). But this is pure speculation!

Korchnoi has a restless streak. His defection from the USSR caused a splash, but he has changed countries twice since then (Holland to Germany to Switzerland) and no one has noticed. He often laments his education in the USSR, but in comparison with Karpov he seems to be a polymath. He has written one book *Chess is My Life* — an inflammatory document and a must for all students of chess current affairs. While playing chess Korchnoi too lives in a world of his own construction. His absolute concentration is aided by deafness which helps him to exclude the external world from his inner consciousness.

Why Baguio?

Why indeed? The Philippines, remote from the centres of western chess life, with its highly spectacular form of personal government in the flamboyant shape of President Marcos, seems an exotic venue for a World Chess Championship. But we should not forget that Manila had first option on the Fischer-Karpov match which did not take place!

For 1978 four realistic bids (prize fund of over 1 million Swiss Francs each) were made to FIDE (the World Chess Federation): Graz (Austria), Hamburg (W. Germany), Tilburg (Holland) and Baguio. Korchnoi's preferences were for Graz, Baguio, Tilburg and Hamburg, in that order, while Karpov put Hamburg first, left second place blank, Baguio third and Graz fourth. FIDE President Euwe then decided on Baguio, and rejected a subsequent offer from Graz and Hamburg to share the match. Karpov is said to have reacted badly to this news. Apparently he only included the Philippines on his list as a political move to exclude Holland, which was Korchnoi's domicile for one year after his defection. Probably he also harbours bad dreams about Manila 1976, one of his worst results as World Champion.

In what follows of Part I, I will attempt to give enough background information for the reader to form his own opinion as to the stature of Karpov and Korchnoi in the historical context of the World Championship, and also to form his own judgement as to their relative merits and respective chances of success. In the section on style I have sought to underline features which may aid appreciation of the games from Baguio.

KARPOV'S PLAYING RECORD

TOURNAMENTS

Year	Event	Place	+	=	−
1966	USSR Junior Championship		4	4	1
	Masters v. Candidate Masters		5	10	0
	Scandinavia Juniors-USSR Juniors	bd. 6	1	1	0
1966/7	Trinec	1st	9	4	0
1967	RSFSR Spartakiad		3	1	1
	USSR Junior Championship, ½ Final	5	3	1	3
1967/8	Groningen	1st	6	8	0
1968	USSR—Yugoslavia	bd. 12	3	1	0
	USSR Juniors—Scandinavia Juniors	bd. 2	0	1	1
	Moscow University Championship	1st	7	6	0
	6th USSR Team Championship	bd. 6	9	2	0
1969	Leningrad Match-Tournament	1st	5	5	2
	USSR Juniors—Yugoslavia Juniors	bd. 3	2	2	0
	USSR Armed Forces Team Championship	bd. 2	5	1	1
	World Junior Championship, Stockholm	1st	12	5	0
	Hungary—RSFSR, Budapest		0	2	2
1970	USSR Armed Forces Team Ch. zonal		3	3	0
	RSFSR Championship, Kuibyshev	1st	8	9	0
	Caracas	4-6	8	7	2
	USSR Armed Forces Team Championship		2	3	1
	38th USSR Championship, Riga	5-7	5	14	2
1971	39th USSR Ch. Daugavpils ½ Final	1st	9	8	0
	Student Olympiad, Mayaguez	bd. 3	7	1	0
	USSR Team Ch. Rostov-on-Don	bd. 6	6	1	0
	USSR Armed Forces Team Championship	bd. 1	2	4	1
	Leningrad University Team Ch.		4	0	0
	39th USSR Ch. Leningrad	4	7	12	2
	Alekhine Memorial, Moscow	1-2	5	12	0
1971/2	Hastings	1-2	8	6	1
1972	USSR Olympiad, Moscow	bd. 2	4	3	2
	Student Olympiad, Graz	bd. 1	5	4	0
	Skopje Olympiad	1st res.	12	2	1
	San Antonio	1-3	7	7	1
1973	Budapest	2nd	4	11	0

	USSR National Teams Match-Tournament	bd. 1	2	2	0
	Leningrad Interzonal	1-2	10	7	0
	European Team Championship, Bath	bd. 4	4	2	0
	41st USSR Championship, Moscow	2-6	5	11	1
	Madrid	1st	7	8	0
1974	Nice Olympiad	bd. 1	10	4	0
1975	Ljubljana—Portoroz	1st	7	8	0
	6th USSR Spartakiad, Riga	bd. 1	4	3	0
	Milan	1st	4	16	1
1976	Skopje	1st	10	5	0
	USSR Cup	bd. 1	2	4	0
	Amsterdam	1st	2	4	0
	Manila	2nd	1	4	1
	Montilla	1st	5	4	0
	44th USSR Championship, Moscow	1st	8	8	1
1977	Bad Lauterberg	1st	9	6	0
	European Team Championship, Moscow	bd. 1	5	0	0
	Las Palmas	1st	12	3	0
	Leningrad	4-5	5	10	2
	Tilburg	1st	5	6	0
1978	Bugojno	1-2	6	8	1

MATCHES

1971	v Korchnoi (training match) Leningrad	drew	2	2	2
1974	v Polugayevsky (Candidates' ¼ Final) Moscow	won	3	5	0
	v Spassky (Candidates' ½ Final) Leningrad	won	4	6	1
	v Korchnoi (Candidates' Final) Moscow	won	3	19	2

Karpov has much less match experience than Korchnoi, but in his brief match career he has been almost uniformly successful. What may prove a handicap to him in Baguio is that he has not yet played a match outside the USSR. Indeed, all of his matches have been in either Moscow or Leningrad.

KORCHNOI'S PLAYING RECORD

TOURNAMENTS

		Place	+	=	−
1946	USSR Junior Ch., Leningrad	11th-12th	4	2	9
1947	USSR Junior Ch., Leningrad	1st	8	7	0
1948	USSR Junior Ch., Tallinn	1st-2nd	5	0	2
1950	Leningrad Ch.	2nd	8	2	3
	½-final 18th USSR Ch., Tula	11th-13th	4	4	7
1951	Chigorin Memorial, Leningrad	5th-7th	6	3	4
	½-final 19th USSR Ch., Leningrad	5th-8th	6	8	4
1952	½-final 20th USSR Ch., Minsk	2nd-4th	7	7	3
	20th USSR Ch., Moscow	6th	8	6	5
	Leningrad Ch.	4th	6	3	4
1953	Leningrad Ch.	2nd	8	3	2
	½-final 21st USSR Ch., Vilnius	3rd-4th	7	4	3
1954	21st USSR Ch. Kiev	2nd-3rd	10	6	3
	Bucharest	1st	10	6	1
	Student Olympiad, Oslo	(board 1)	3	3	1
	½-final 22nd USSR Ch., Erevan	3rd-5th	9	8	3
1955	22nd USSR Ch., Moscow	19th	1	10	8
	½-final 23rd USSR Ch., Riga	4th-5th	8	6	4
	Leningrad Ch.	1st	16	2	1
	Hastings (1955/6)	1st-2nd	5	4	0
1956	23rd USSR Ch., Leningrad	4th	6	10	1
	Student Olympiad, Uppsala	(board 1)	5	2	0
	½-final 24th USSR Ch., Tbilisi	3rd-4th	7	10	2
1957	Leningrad Ch.	1st-2nd	11	4	2
	24th USSR Ch., Moscow	7th-8th	6	12	3
	Armenian Ch. (hors concours)	1st			
	European Team Ch., Vienna	(board 8)	5	1	0
	½-final 25th USSR Ch., Sverdlovsk	1st	8	11	0
1958	25th USSR Ch., Riga	9th-11th	4	9	4
	RSFSR Ch., Sochi	2nd-4th	7	10	2
	½-final 26th USSR Ch., Tashkent	2nd-3rd	9	4	2
1959	26th USSR Ch., Tbilisi	9th	6	8	5
	Krakow	1st	6	5	0
	½-final 27th USSR Ch., Cheliabinsk	1st	9	6	0

1960	27th USSR Ch., Leningrad	1st	12	4	3
	Moscow	3rd	6	4	1
	Buenos Airies	1st-2nd	9	8	2
	Santa Fe	4th	3	3	1
	Corboda	1st	5	2	0
	Leipzig Olympiad	(board 4)	8	5	0
	28th USSR Ch., Moscow	2nd	9	8	2
	European Team Ch., Oberhausen	(board 3)	8	1	0
	Budapest	1st	9	5	1
1962	Interzonal Stockholm	4th-5th	9	10	3
	Candidates' Tournament, Curacao	5th	7	13	7
	30th USSR Ch., Erevan	1st	8	1	1
1963	Havana	1st	14	5	2
	31st USSR Ch., Leningrad	10th	4	12	3
1964	Leningrad Ch.	1st	12	4	0
	Zonal Tournament, Moscow	5th-6th	3	5	4
	Belgrade	2nd-3rd	9	5	2
	32nd USSR Ch., Kiev (1964/5)	1st	11	8	0
1965	European Team Ch., Hamburg	(board 3)	4	3	2
	Gyula	1st	14	1	0
	Erevan	1st	6	7	0
	33rd USSR Ch., Tallinn	10th-12th	6	6	7
1966	Training Tournament, Moscow	4th-5th	2	4	4
	Bucharest	1st	11	3	0
	Sochi	1st	10	3	2
	USSR Team Ch., Moscow	(board 2)	5	5	0
	Havana Olympiad	(board 5)	9	3	1
	34th USSR Ch., Tbilisi (1966/7)	3rd-5th	4	16	0
1967	Play-off for Interzonal, Tallinn	1st-3rd	1	2	1
	Leningrad	1st	10	6	0
	Interzonal Tournament, Sousse	2nd-4th	9	10	3
1968	Wijk aan Zee	1st	10	4	1
	Lugano Olympiad	(board 3)	9	4	0
	Palma de Mallorca	1st	11	6	0
1969	Sarajevo	1st	9	6	0
	Luhacovice	1st	8	7	0
	Havana	1st-2nd	8	6	1
	Palma de Mallorca	3rd-4th	6	9	2
1970	USSR vs Rest of the World, Belgrade	(board 3)	0	3	1
	Rovini/Zagreb	2nd-5th	7	8	2
	European Team Ch., Kapfenberg	(board 2)	2	4	0
	Siegen Olympiad	(board 3)	8	6	1*
	38th USSR Ch., Riga	1st	12	8	1
1971	Wijk aan Zee	1st	7	6	2
	Moscow	11th	6	5	6
	Hastings (1971/2)	1st-2nd	8	6	1

1972	Amsterdam	2nd	7	8	0
	Skopje Olympiad	(board 2)	8	6	1
	Palma de Mallorca	1st-3rd	7	6	2
1973	Leningrad Ch.	8th-9th	5	4	5
	Interzonal, Leningrad	1st-2nd	11	5	1
	European Team Ch., Bath	(board 3)	3	2	1
	41st USSR Ch., Moscow	2nd-6th	5	11	1
1974	Nice Olympiad	(board 2)	8	7	0
1975	Moscow	3rd-5th	8	3	4
	Hastings (1975/76)	4th	5	8	2
1976	Amsterdam	1st-2nd	5	9	1
1977	Montreux	1st	4	5	0
	Dutch Ch., Leeuwarden	1st	11	2	0
1978	Wijk aan Zee	2nd	5	5	1
	Beer-Sheva	1st	11	2	0

* Korchnoi overslept and lost against Spain by default

MATCHES

1968	v Reshevsky (Candidates' ¼-final), Amsterdam	won	3	5	0
	v Tal (Candidates' ½-final), Moscow	won	2	7	1
	v Spassky (Candidates' final), Kiev	lost	1	5	4
1970	v Bronstein (training match)	lost	1	2	3
1971	v Karpov (training match), Leningrad	drew	2	2	2
	v Geller (Candidates' ¼-final), Moscow	won	4	3	1
	v Petrosian (Candidates' ½-final), Moscow	lost	0	9	1
1974	v Mecking (Candidates' ¼-final), Augusta	won	3	9	1
	v Petrosian (Candidates' ½-final), Odessa	won	3	1	1
	v Karpov (Candidates Final)	lost	2	19	3
1976	v Timman, Leeuwarden	won	4	3	1
	v Hug, Zurich	won	2	2	0
1977	v Petrosian (Candidates' ¼-final), Lucca	won	2	9	1
	v Polugayevsky (Candidates' ½-final), Evian	won	5	7	1
	v Spassky (Candidates' final) Belgrade	won	7	7	4

4

A HISTORY
OF THE
WORLD CHAMPIONSHIP

If you were to ask an ordinary citizen whether he knew more about Morphy or Smyslov (or whether he had even heard of Smyslov), I am sure I know which answer would be returned — yet Smyslov was World Champion for one year, while Morphy was merely a legendary chess genius, with no official title. The official World Championships began with the Steinitz-Zukertort match of 1886, yet before that time there were many talented players who merited the accolade of a World title which did not yet exist. The most prominent amongst these were the Frenchmen, Philidor and Labourdonnais, the Englishman, Staunton, Adolph Anderssen a German, and Morphy himself, from the New World. But it took a shrewd Austrian Jew, Wilhelm Steinitz, to invent the official title, and so his name appears first on the official roll of honour.

Wilhelm Steinitz (Austria)	1886-1894
Emmanuel Lasker (Germany)	1894-1921
Jose Raul Capablanca (Cuba)	1921-1927
Alexander Alekhine (Russia and France)	1927-1935
Max Euwe (Holland)	1935-1937
Alexander Alekhine	1937-1946
Mikhail Botvinnik (USSR)	1948-1957
Vassily Smyslov (USSR)	1957-1958
Mikhail Botvinnik	1958-1960
Mikhail Tal (USSR)	1960-1961
Mikhail Botvinnik	1961-1963
Tigran Petrosian (USSR)	1963-1969
Boris Spassky (USSR)	1969-1972
Robert Fischer (USA)	1972-1975
Anatoly Karpov (USSR)	1975-??

Until the death of Alekhine the destination of the supreme title depended on free enterprise. There was no way of compelling the reigning champion to defend his title but the twin incentives of honour and money ensured that he did so with reasonable frequency. Nobody had an automatic right to challenge the champion but anyone who seemed to have a reasonable chance of unseating him was liable to be able to find suitable sponsors.

The free enterprise system did not work too badly but there were justifiable criticisms of it. Some title matches resulted in rather pointless laps of honour for the champion and were held merely because the challenger had suitable financial backing rather than because he had any real chance of winning. Some matches which the chess world would have loved to witness never took place either because the potential challenger was unable to find suitable backing or (some people claimed) because the champion deliberately avoided the encounter by demanding unreasonable terms.

When Alekhine died in harness in 1946 the world chess organisation, FIDE, leapt at the opportunity to assume control of the world championship. They solved the immediate problem of ending the interregnum created by Alekhine's death by organising a tournament (won by Botvinnik) in which the five best players in the world played each other five times. Thereafter FIDE decreed that the champion must defend his title every three years against a challenger selected by a comprehensive system of elimination tournaments. The 'three year rule' should have been sufficient to ensure that the champion did not rest on his laurels and that any defeated champion had an opportunity to regain his title. But FIDE also decreed that a defeated champion should be entitled to a return match within one year. This rule (nicknamed 'the Botvinnik rule' because he twice benefited from it) was manifestly unfair because there was no provision for a 'return return' match and so the champion had two bites at the cherry but the challenger didn't. The Botvinnik rule was dropped in 1963.

Until FIDE took over, the conditions for world championship matches were decided by negotiation between the players and their sponsors. Sometimes the match was the best of a fixed number of games and sometimes it was decided by the first player to win a fixed number of games. Matches varied in length from ten games (Lasker-Schlechter 1910) to thirty-five (Capablanca-Alekhine 1927). FIDE standardised the format by decreeing that every match should be for the best of twenty-four games with the champion retaining is title in the event of a tie.

The FIDE system worked smoothly until the arrival of that strong-willed genius, Fischer on the scene. Negotiations for his match against Spassky 1972 almost broke down and in 1975 negotiations for his match with Karpov actually did break down and Karpov was declared champion by default. Fischer has threatened to go over the heads of FIDE and play an unofficial world championship match. This would seriously undermine the authority of FIDE and result in the unsatisfactory existence of two 'world champions' — one official, the other not. So far this danger has been averted.

The clock was put back in two ways for the 1978 match. The 'Botvinnik' return match rule was reintroduced and the match was to go to the first player to win six games. Both these changes were criticised but at least there was general relief that the best two active players in the world had agreed on a set of rules and a world championship match would take place for the first time in six years.

5

KARPOV'S
RECORD AS
WORLD CHAMPION

World Champions are not just in competition with their contemporaries, they also have to maintain their historical record against their predecessors and successors in the championship. If we compare Karpov with the eleven former World Champions we see that he has now moved into the lead as regards the number of undivided first prizes in major tournaments obtained throughout their respective tenures. Here is the evidence of each champion, and the number of important firsts he gained in his championship period:

Steinitz 0; Lasker 5; Capablanca 2; Alekhine 5; Euwe 0; Botvinnik 0; Smyslov 0; Tal 0; Petrosian 0; Spassky 1; Fischer 0; Karpov 7.

Karpov's victories were: Ljubljana—Portorozh 1975; Milan 1975; Skopje 1976; USSR Championship 1976; Bad Lauterberg 1977; Las Palmas 1977 and Tilburg 1977.

Tournaments aside, Lasker defended his title successfully in six matches, Steinitz in three, Alekhine and Botvinnik twice, and Petrosian once. All the others shed their title at the first challenge, with the exception of Fischer who let his title go by default. Fischer's reign was, in fact, the most miserable of all, since he played only one game, and this an 'exhibition' draw of no importance against President Marcos of the Philippines. Incredibly, no World Champion won undivided first prize in a major tournament between Alekhine and Spassky. Alekhine's last great victory was Zurich 1934, although I have been generous and allowed him the less impressive Nazi-inspired 'European Championship' at Munich 1942 to build up his total of five.

Karpov's record certainly seems to put most other World Champions to shame, but we have to remember that Karpov started with one big advantage as World Champion: he did not have to play a World Championship match to gain his title! This meant that he had huge reserves of untapped energy to expend on tournament successes — reserves which must have been denied to Euwe, for example, who had to contest 30 tough games with Alekhine, or to Spassky, who had to fight two gruelling matches with Petrosian. On top of this, there is the question of unsatisfied ambition. The majority of World Champions must surely believe that they have proved themselves and need no further self-justification. There must even be a temptation to relax, having achieved the highest title. But

Karpov did not prove himself to be the best player — Fischer merely failed to turn up. So Karpov had to provide the proof himself in tournaments by battering all prospective opposition and critics into silence. After his victories in seven major tournaments, his share of first prize in the super-tournament at Bugojno 1978, and a host of fine performances in lesser events, no one can possibly regard Karpov as a paper tiger, or indeed, as anything less than a worthy and active successor to Fischer's title.

KARPOV'S SCORE AGAINST THE OTHER WORLD CHAMPIONS

Karpov's Score	Won	Drawn	Lost
Euwe	0	0	0
Botvinnik	0	1	0
Smyslov	1	6	1
Tal	0	11	0
Petrosian	0	10	1
Spassky	6	11	2
Fischer	0	0	0
Total	7	39	4

Karpov has 26½ points from 50 games (53 per cent) against the other World Champions he has played.

6

KORCHNOI'S
PATH TO THE
WORLD CHAMPIONSHIP

Towards the end of 1974 Victor Korchnoi succumbed, by the narrowest of margins, to Anatoly Karpov in the Final of the Ninth Candidates' Tournament, which was held in Moscow. The final score of this mammoth struggle was 3 wins to Karpov, 2 wins to Korchnoi and 19 draws. Korchnoi has since claimed that for this contest the Soviet authorities favoured his opponent as the younger man, one who had never met Fischer, or been defeated by him, and who would therefore maintain a more credible image as World Champion if, or when, Fischer failed to show for the title match. Consequently, Korchnoi found it almost impossible to obtain grandmasterly assistance and was constantly subjected to threats and harassment. Anyone who has read the Panovs' account of their life at the Kirov Ballet, after they had applied for exit visas to Israel, will readily comprehend what is meant by this. Korchnoi personally went through the galling experience of seeing an army of the best Soviet chess brains ranged against him.

The Soviet calculation turned out to be correct and Fischer, foundering in a morass of his own 'principles', ceded the World Championship to Karpov without play, early in 1975. But what of Korchnoi? Some unnecessarily sharp remarks he made about Karpov had earned him an even less justifiable banishment from chess tournaments lasting one year. So, while Karpov toured the globe as a conquering hero, Korchnoi had to sit in his home town of Leningrad, twiddling his thumbs and waiting . . . .

Korchnoi is a man of decision. Realising that he could no longer gain his ultimate ambition (the World Championship) in a Soviet context, he resolved to free himself at the earliest opportunity. After a year's 'detention' Korchnoi finally began to receive invitations to foreign tournaments again, and, seizing his chance at the end of the IBM competition at Amsterdam in the summer of 1976, he walked into a police station and requested 'political asylum'. This was less an act of political defiance than a professional gesture. If Korchnoi wished to pursue his goal he had to leave the USSR. A leading professional chess grandmaster cannot risk a sudden and arbitrarily imposed banning at a critical stage of his career if he wants to fight for the World Championship!

By virtue of his second place in the 1974 Candidates' Korchnoi had won the right to compete again in 1977, but the Soviet Federation was quick to strike back, by demanding from FIDE that Korchnoi be expelled from the tournament and thus excluded from participation in the World Championship. To the honour of FIDE, and the President Dr Max Euwe, this request was refused and Korchnoi proceeded to the 10th Candidates' Tournament.

The 10th Candidates' Cycle, 1977-1978

The knock-out has been in force ever since 1965, when the all-play-all was dropped after Fischer's allegations of 'Commie cheating'.

Quarter-Final matches were for the best of 12 games; Semi-Finals out of 16 and the Final out of 20. There was a provision (actually invoked for Hort-Spassky) for further 2 game mini-matches if deadlock was reached.

¼-Final		½-Final		Final		
Korchnoi (Stateless)	6½					
Petrosian (USSR)	5½	**Korchnoi**	8½			
Polugayevsky (USSR)	6½	Polugayevsky	4½			
Mecking (Brazil)	5½			**Korchnoi**	10½	**Korchnoi**
Spassky (USSR)	8½			Spassky	7½	
Hort (Czechoslovakia)	7½	**Spassky**	8½			
Portisch (Hungary)	6½	Portisch	6½			
Larsen (Denmark)	3½					

Details of Korchnoi's matches are given below:

Quarter Finals

Il Ciocca 1977

Korchnoi	½	½	½	½	1	0	½	1	½	½	½	½	6½
Petrosian	½	½	½	½	0	1	½	0	½	½	½	½	5½

This was Korchnoi's first serious test since his defection, and, ironically, he was drawn against his arch-enemy Petrosian. I will confine comments to Korchnoi's own remarks from *Chess is My Life*.

It was an agonizing experience and in the newspapers they called it the 'match of hate'. We did not speak to each other, did not shake each other's hand, did not allow our gaze to cross. Through the arbiter, Kazic, a draw was offered. It was as well that the chessboard was the only battlefield. My nerves were, however, somewhat stronger. The standard of play was awfully low. In the difficult circumstances mistake just followed mistake.

Hardly an auspicious start for Korchnoi!

Semi-Finals

Evian 1977

Korchnoi	1	1	1	½	½	1	1	0	½	½	½	½	½		8½
Polugayevsky	0	0	0	½	½	0	0	1	½	½	½	½	½		4½

In 1974 I visited Korchnoi in Moscow, during a particularly black patch of his match with Karpov. At that stage he was trailing by 3 points but friendly support (from myself and the Hartstons) helped him to recover, and he even used one of my ideas in the Queen's Indian to win the 21st game. Ever since that time I had the feeling that I could co-operate with him, but the opportunity did not arise until his defection from the USSR. At the Montreux tournament (immediately after his match with Petrosian) Korchnoi invited me to act as his second, an offer which I was delighted to accept. I then recruited Michael Stean to join Korchnoi's squad.

As can be seen, the course of the match was a disaster for the Soviet side — one of the most crushing Candidates' results since Fischer's rampage in 1971. During the match I was pleasantly surprised by the standard of the much-vaunted Soviet adjournment analysis, which became so feeble that we were always confident of getting the right result if a game was adjourned. We knew it wouldn't be so easy against Karpov!

Acting as Korchnoi's second gave me some fascinating insights into the petty political manoeuvres the official Russians were prepared to indulge in to demoralise the opposition. It took me two days of negotiation with V.D. Baturinsky (leader of the Soviet delegation) before they would even agree to let Polugayevsky shake hands at the start of each game, and they were adamant about refusing Korchnoi a flag under which to play. Personally, I believe that Korchnoi is proud of his 'statelessness' and at the preliminary meetings I proposed that Korchnoi play under the 'Skull and Crossbones', but you can guess the answer to that.

Final

Belgrade 1977/78

Korchnoi	½	1	1	½	½	½	1	1	½	1	0	0	0	0	½	½	1	1	10½
Spassky	½	0	0	½	½	½	0	0	½	0	1	1	1	1	½	½	0	0	7½

It is clear from the scores of this match that something very unusual occurred after the 10th game, when Korchnoi's winning margin of 5 points was cut to almost nothing, in a dramatic and virtually unprecedented reversal of fortune. There has been too much speculation concerning parapsychology, death rays, black magic and witchcraft surrounding this contest, but in my opinion the strange events can mainly be explained by nervous tension. Spassky spent the second half of the match planning his moves from a closed box off-stage and indulging in other semi-legal behaviour. Korchnoi became infected by this artificially strained atmosphere, but he eventually recovered his poise to secure a substantial and well-deserved victory.

Facts and Figures

In order to challenge Karpov for the World Championship Korchnoi had to play 43 games in the Candidates' Tournament, of which he won 14, lost 6 and drew 23. This comes to 25½ points or 59.89 per cent. Of his 14 wins 7 were with Black.

Let us compare that with Karpov's performance in the 1974 Candidates', when his defeat of Korchnoi earned him the abortive right to meet Fischer. Karpov also played 43 games, winning 10 losing 3 and drawing 30 (25 points or 58.14 per cent). Karpov only won 2 games with Black, but these 2 included the 17th game of the Final which broke Korchnoi's serve and provided Karpov with his decisive extra point.

The records of the two in their respective Candidates' Tournaments are almost equal, but Karpov had made tremendous progress since he became World Champion, so much so, in fact, that several experts (including Tony Miles in the *New Statesman*) were predicting one year ago that the 1978 World Championship would be a no-contest. The irony of Karpov's position in 1975 was that he was universally regarded as second best to Fischer, an assessment which he could not disprove, in spite of his own willingness to play against the American Grandmaster. In compensation, Karpov ran up a truly amazing series of tournament successes, but Korchnoi has also performed with terrible force since his near-fiasco against Petrosian, and we can now look forward to that rare phenomenon — a World Championship with both players in peak form.

7

KARPOV'S STYLE

One senses sacrilege in the air when speaking of Karpov and style in the same breath, since Karpov is a near-perfect player who almost rises above stylistic considerations. Nevertheless, Karpov still exhibits certain subtle preferences, there are still certain operations which he carries out with greater or lesser degrees of dexterity, and he has certain characteristics which any prospective opponent would examine in detail.

The hallmark of Karpov's games is fluency and ease. He is the Mozart of the chessboard and in chess terms he enjoys Capablanca's speed of play, the invincibility of Petrosian in his best days and the killer instinct of Fischer. This killer instinct is not expressed by any overt show of tempestuous aggression but by a machine-like insistence which gradually wears down the most stubborn of opponents.

The strengths (and possible weakness) of Karpov's style can be more easily defined under four headings:-

Speed of Play

If one examines the 24 games played between Karpov and Korchnoi in their 1974 match it becomes obvious that Karpov was by far the more rapid player. Only Capablanca in his prime played so consistently fast in important matches. Very rarely Karpov's speed leads to superficial decisions, but in the practical struggle it usually turns out to be a devastating weapon which leaves the opponent floundering in time-trouble. Against Olafsson at Bad Lauterberg 1977 Karpov had used 2¼ hours after 2 sessions of play, while the Icelandic Grandmaster had consumed 5¼ hours. In the *New Statesman* Tony Miles asked whether the time difference at the end of that game was a record for modern chess.

To illustrate Karpov's speed of play here is his rapid demolition of Lajos Portisch, rated at that time at 2625.

Portisch — Karpov, King's Indian Attack, Europa Cup, Moscow 1977

1 N-KN3	N-KB3
2 P-KN3	P-QN3
3 B-N2	B-N2
4 0-0	P-K3
5 P-Q3	

It is a matter of taste, but I think 5 P-B4 is more active.

| 5 ... | P-Q4 |
| 6 QN-Q2 | QN-Q2 |

7 R-K1   B-B4

Fluid development is typical of Karpov's style but one cannot deny the originality of developing the KB at QB4 in a Flank Opening.

8 P-B4

This shows that Portisch had been driven into a passive frame of mind by the prospect of facing the World Champion. The consistent course now is 8 P-K3 (to blunt the operation of Black's KB) followed by the fianchetto of White's QB.

8 . . .	0-0
9 PxP	PxP
10 N-N3	B-N5
11 B-Q2	P-QR4

More ambitious than 11 . . . BxB 12 QxB P-QB4 which would have been good enough for equality.

12 QN-Q4	R-K1
13 QR-B1	P-B4
14 N-B5	N-B1
15 P-Q4?	

Provoking a sharp struggle at the wrong moment.

| 15 . . . | N-K5 |
| 16 PxP? | |

White's position is already bad but this is a blunder losing material.

| 16 . . . | NxB |

17 NxN   Q-N4!

Forking White's knights. If now 18 N-K3 RxN 19 PxR QxP+ wins.

18 N-Q6	BxN
19 NxB	BxR(K8)
20 QxB	RxP
21 QxR	QxR+
22 Q-B1	Q-Q7
23 PxP	R-QB1

White Resigns.

I was playing on top board for England in this event and during my game with Smejkal our deliberations were rudely interrupted by an explosion of cheering and shouting in the tournament hall. It transpired that Karpov had crushed Portisch and the crowd was registering its appreciation. I wandered over to their board and looked at the clock-times: Portisch had taken 2 hours and 10 minutes. If his position had not been bad enough to resign then he would soon have found himself in time-trouble. I then looked at Karpov's clock. He had taken just 1 hour to annihilate a semifinalist from the Candidates' tournament!

Precision of Calculation

At nearly all times Karpov sees his way very clearly. He holds the structure of future events in his mind, rather like Michelangelo, who claimed he could see the future shape of his sculpture in the rough block of stone. Many people regard Karpov as an icy calculating machine without nerves, and he exerts an impressive personal power precisely because he is so calm and controlled.

As an example of this I want to cite his game against Miles from Tilburg 1977. The English Grandmaster caught Karpov in a sharp prepared variation, which involved a rook sacrifice to trap the White king in the centre of the board — now read on . . .

Karpov — Miles, English Opening, Tilburg 1977

1 P-QB4 P-QB4 2 N-KB3 N-KB3 3 N-B3 N-B3 4 P-Q4 PxP 5 NxP P-K3 6 P-KN3 Q-N3 7 N-N3 N-K4 8 P-K4 B-N5 9 Q-K2 P-QR4 10 B-K3 Q-B3 11 P-B3 0-0 12 N-Q4 Q-R3 13 N-N5 P-Q4

Miles had had this position once before in 1977. Then he was White against Nunn in a game from the 2nd T.V. Master Game Tournament and the game had continued: 14 BPxP PxP 15 B-Q4 PxP 16 BxN PxP 17 Q-B4 P-B7+ 18 K-Q1 R-Q1+ 19 K-B1 B-K3 with obscure complications which ended in a draw. Watch how Karpov wields his intellectual machete to cut his way through the tangled jungle of variations.

    14 N-B7!   Q-Q3

The alternative is 14 . . . Q-B3 when Karpov gives the following plausible main line: 15 NxR Nx

QBP 16 B-Q4 P-K4 17 PxP NxQP 18 QxN PxB 19 QxQ PxQ 20 P-QR3 PxN 21 PxB BPxP 22 R-QN1 PxP 23 RxP B-B4 24 N-N6! NxN 25 RxP and White has the superior ending.

    15 NxR   **PxKP**

  More complicated is 15 . . . Nx QBP. After the text Black's attack fizzles out.

    16 PxP   **NxKP**
    17 R-Q1   **Q-B3**
    18 B-N2   **NxBP**
    19 B-Q4   **BxN+**
    20 PxB   **P-B4**
    21 0—0   **N/B5-Q3**
    22 N-N6   **P-K4**
    23 NxB   **RxN**
    24 BxKP   **Q-B4+**
    25 B-Q4
    Black Resigns.

Virtuoso in Space

Ever since the days of Dr Tarrasch any strong player knows how to cramp the opposing position with pawns, if given the opportunity. Karpov, however, has mastered the difficult art of maintaining, and consistently exploiting, a space advantage in fluid, open positions *by piece control alone*. This is a particularly striking facet of his style which I will illustrate with a thematic game against the Soviet Grandmaster Mark Taimanov.

Karpov — Taimanov, Sicilian Defence, USSR Team Championship, Moscow 1972.

1 P-K4 P-QB4 2 N-KB3 P-K3 3 P-Q4 PxP 4 NxP P-QR3 5 B-Q3 B-B4

6 N-N3 B-N3 7 0-0 N-K2 8 Q-K2
QN-B3   9 B-K3 N-K4   10 P-QB4
BxB   11 QxB Q-B2   12 P-B5!

The first step in a strategy designed to dominate the dark squares.

12 ...   NxB
13 QxN   P-QN3

Black immediately takes measures to challenge the advanced pawn, but even after it has disappeared it leaves a strong square for White in its wake.

14 PxP   QxNP
15 N/1-Q2   P-Q4
16 P-K5!

Although this gives Black a passed pawn it increases White's network of dark square domination.

16 ...   B-Q2
17 KR—B1   0-0
18 Q-Q4

Methodically driving Black back. After 18 . . . QxQ 19 NxQ KR-B1 20 N/2-N3 N-B3 21 NxN BxN 22 N-Q4 White enjoys a favourable ending.

18 ...   Q-N1
19 N-B3   N-B3
20 Q-K3   R-B1
21 R-B5   P-QR4
22 R/1-QB1   P-R5
23 N/N3-Q4   N-R4

Black does everything he can to achieve Q-side counterplay. His threat of . . . N-B5 forces White to isolate his QNP.

24 RxR+   BxR
25 P-QN3   B-Q2
26 P-R4   P-R3
27 P-KN4!

The manoeuvre inaugurated by the text goes beyond a mere technical exploitation of a spatial plus. Karpov not only uses his central grip to defend his potentially shaky Q-side, but also to launch a sudden raid against the Black king. White's QR, innocently controlling a Q-side file is, in fact, destined to join in an attack on the other side of the board.

27 ...   Q-N2
28 P-R5   N-B3
29 P-N5   NxN
30 NxN   KRPxP
31 QxP

Threatening P-R6.

31 ...   K-R2
32 R-B3   Q-N5
33 R-N3   R-KN1
34 N-B3   PxP
35 PxP   QxP

DIAGRAM

The culmination of Black's Q-side

24

initiative — he wins the isolated pawn. Unfortunately, White has been given sufficient time to build up a mating attack.

36 Q-B1	Q-R7
37 N-N5+	K-R1
38 NxP+	K-R2
39 Q-N5	Q-N8+
40 K-R2	Resigns.

There is no defence to Q-N6+.

Karpov's Weakness

If Karpov has a weakness it is a slight hesitancy when faced by unusual openings, often of the old-fashioned, classical variety. I exploited this in my game against Karpov from Bad Lauterberg 1977 by playing the virtually unexplored Philidor Defence against him.

Karpov scored 7½/8 with White in that tournament, and my game was the half. As further evidence here is a rather unconvincing Karpov draw with this kind of opening against an opponent Karpov would normally expect to beat.

Haase — Karpov, Centre Game, Skopje Olympiad 1972

1 P-K4 P-K4 2 P-Q4 PxP 3 QxP N-QB3 4 Q-K3 P-Q3 5 N-QB3 N-B3 6 B-Q2 B-K2 7 0-0-0 0-0 8 Q-N3 P-QR3 9 P-B4 P-QN4 10 P-K5 N-Q2 11 N-B3 R-N1 12 N-Q5 N-B4 13 B-K3 N-K5 14 Q-K1 P-B4 15 P-KR3 B-K3 16 R-N1 K-R1 17 P-KN4 PxP 18 NxB QxN 19 Nx P NxN 20 PxN R/N1-Q1 21 B-Q3 B-Q4 **Drawn**

8
KORCHNOI'S STYLE

Most of what has been written about Korchnoi's style (including some remarks of my own which appeared at the time of the 1974 match) is now hopelessly out of date. Usually one reads about the heroic defender in hectic time-trouble, the veins on his brow bursting with his immense will to win, always ready to snatch material and weather the attack etc. . . Probably this was the stereotyped impression Spassky had of him before their match in Belgrade last year.

The keynotes are still striving and determination, but Korchnoi's style has rounded and developed in remarkable fashion since he came to the West. He has successfully eliminated that drop of poison which vitiated his earlier achievements. He now avoids time-trouble if possible, instead of revelling in it, as he seemed to do in former times, and he no longer overestimates material in relation to the initiative. Indeed, he has developed a very fine feeling for the initiative and is particularly dangerous with Black, when he sees the chance to offer a pawn sacrifice early in the game to disorganise his opponent's position. In this respect he bears comparison with Alekhine, as well as with his own hero, the Apostle of the Struggle, Emanuel Lasker.

I will illustrate these points with two of his games from the 1977 Candidates' cycle.

Polugayevsky — Korchnoi, English Defence, Evian 1977 (Game 6)

1 P-Q4	P-K3
2 P-QB4	P-QN3
3 P-K4	

Played with an air of disbelief by Polugayevsky who obviously regarded Black's formation as a bad joke.

3 . . .	B-N2
4 Q-B2	

Polugayevsky's idea is to defend his KP without playing N-QB3 which would risk doubled pawns after . . . B-N5.

| 4 . . . | Q-R5! |

26

An unpleasant surprise for Polugayevsky and one which appears
to break a number of sound, ele-
mentary rules. However, it is surprisingly difficult to drive away
the annoying Black queen.

5 N-Q2

Nineteen minutes spent over this,
so Black's strange opening was already justified in a practical sense.

5 . . .	B-N5
6 B-Q3	P-KB4
7 N-B3	BxN+
8 K-B1?	

Feeble. To be consistent White
must sacrifice two pawns with 8
BxB Q-N5 9 N-K5! QxNP 10 0-0-
0 PxP 11 B-K2 when vast complications ensue. After the text White
gains a pawn but he loses the right
to castle and also allows his pawn
structure to be ruined.

8 . . .	Q-R4
9 BxB	N-KB3
10 PxP	BxN
11 PxB	N-B3
12 B-B3	0-0
13 R-K1	Q-R6+

Significantly preferring pursuit
of the attack to re-establishment
of material equality with 13 . . .
QxBP.

14 K-K2	QR-K1
15 K-Q1	P-K4!

DIAGRAM

Spurning pawns, Korchnoi intro-
duces an imaginative combination
which exploits the shaky position
of White's king in the middle of
the board. I must say, the position
at the moment looks like a reversed
King's Gambit, where everything
has gone wrong for White.

16 PxP	NxP
17 B-K2	

Or 17 BxN RxB 18 RxR QxP+
and . . . QxR.

17 . . .	NxKBP!

The point of Black's play.

18 Q-Q3	RxB
19 RxR	

If 19 KxR Q-R4 and Black wins.

19 . . .	Q-N7
20 KR-K1	NxR
21 KxN	QxRP?

Jeopardising victory. By interpos-
ing 21 . . . Q-N8+ 22 K-Q2 and
only then . . . QxRP Korchnoi
could have prevented the invasion
of his position which now occurs.

22 R-K7	Q-N8+
23 K-K2	Q-N5+
24 K-K1	P-KR4
25 Q-N3!	

A difficult decision to make, but
it is the right one. Exchange of
queens eases the task of defence.
From now until the adjournment
Polugayevsky plays excellently
and brings about a drawish ending.

25 . . . QxQ 26 PxQ R-B2 27 BxN
PxB 28 R-K8+ K-N2 29 K-B2 K-
R3 30 P-QN4 K-N4 31 R-QR8 Kx
P 32 RxP P-Q3 33 P-R4 K-K3 34
P-R5 PxP 35 RxRP P-KB4 36 P-B5

R-R2 37 PxP PxP 38 P-N5 P-R5
39 PxP RxP 40 R-R8 R-QN5 41
R-QN8 K-Q4

The adjourned position. Polugayevsky seemed to be anxious to
set up some kind of time record
for sealed moves since he now
consumed 51 minutes, leaving himself just over 8 minutes for 14
moves nex day.

Our adjournment analysis was
not particularly fruitful. Of course,
we did not know Polugayevsky's
sealed move and we could find
nothing very convincing against
42 R-N6!; 42 K-B3 also seemed
impossible to crack by orthodox
methods.

42 K-B3   R-N6+!?

A psychological blow. It looks
nonsensical to free White's king,
but Korchnoi was relying on the
fact that Polugayevsky would
probably have analysed more
'dangerous' tries. With only 8
minutes until move 56 there was
plenty of scope for error, even
against 'nonsense'.

43 K-B4   K-B4
44 R-QB8+?

The losing check. The immediate
KxP should draw. Korchnoi now
played his remaining moves in-
stantly, so that Polugayevsky had
no time to think at all.

44 . . . KxP 45 KxP R-K6 46 K-B4
R-K8 47 R-Q8 K-B4 48 R-QB8+
K-Q5 49 K-B3 P-Q4 50 K-B2 R-K4
51 R-QR8 K-B6 52 R-R3+ K-N5
53 R-R1 P-Q5 54 R-QB1 P-Q6 55
R-B8 P-Q7 56 R-QN8+ K-B6 57 R-
QB8+ K-Q6 58 R-Q8+ K-B7 59 R-
QB8+ K-Q8 White Resigned.

It is apparent from this game that
Korchnoi is also a great master of
the endgame. In fact, from my
own experience of his endgame
analysis, I would say that he is
fully the equal of all the practi-
tioners in this branch of the art of
chess, both from the past and in
the present day. His psychological
approach to the question of the
adjourned position is also worthy
of deep study.

Spassky — Korchnoi, French
Defence, Belgrade 1977, Game 2
1 P-K4 P-K3 2 P-Q4 P-Q4 3 N-QB3
B-N5 4 P-K5 P-QB4 5 P-QR3 BxN+
6 PxB N-K2 7 Q-N4 PxP 8 QxNP
R-N1 9 QxRP Q-B2 10 N-K2 QN-
B3 11 P-KB4 B-Q2 12 Q-Q3 PxP
13 B-K3 P-Q5!

Korchnoi had specially prepared this sharp line as a psychological weapon. Black seizes the initiative at the cost of one or two pawns — extremely uncongenial for Spassky who prefers attack to defence.

14 B-B2	0-0-0
15 NxQP	NxN
16 QxN	P-N3
17 B-R4	B-N4
18 Q-K4	BxB
19 RxB?	

Spassky could have drawn with 19 Q-R8+ K-Q2 (19 . . . Q-N1 is too risky) 20 0-0-0+ N-Q4 21 Rx N+ PxR 22 QxQ—+ K-B1 23 Q-R8+ etc.

19 . . .	R-Q4
20 BxN	QxB
21 R-B3	K-N1
22 K-B1	

If 22 RxP Q-R5+ 23 K-B1 R-Q7 is unpleasant. A significant improvement is 22 P-N3! e.g. 22 . . . R-Q7 23 R-P RxRP 24 0-0-0, as pointed out by Najdorf.

22 . . .	R-Q7
23 R-B2	R(1)-Q1
24 Q-B3	RxR+
25 KxR	R-Q7+
26 K-N3	

Or 26 K-B1 Q-B4 with advantage to Black.

26 . . .	Q-Q1

Although White is a pawn ahead his defence is hampered by the insecure position of his king. Note that 26 . . . RxBP 27 Q-Q3 gives Black nothing but now he threatens to capture on QB7.

27 Q-K4	Q-N1+
28 K-R3	Q-R1+
29 K-N3	Q-N2+

30 K-R3	R-Q1

Threatening mate. Now Black's queen and rook develop amazing versatility and hammer White from all directions.

31 P-N4	R-R1+
32 K-N3	Q-R3
33 Q-N2	Q-R5+
34 K-B3	R-Q1
35 Q-N3	Q-K2
36 P-N5?	

In time-trouble Spassky lets slip his last chance, 36 R-K1.

36 . . .	R-Q7
37 K-N4	Q-N2
38 QxP	R-N7+
39 K-R3	R-B7
40 K-N4	Q-K5

White Resigns.

To encapsulate the contrast in style between Karpov and Korchnoi I would say it was a matter of Fluency v Dynamism. We know that Karpov has always admired Capablanca, while Korchnoi looks to Lasker for inspiration and I have compared his recent games to those of Alekhine. So, the question is — will Baguio 1978 be a repetition of Capablanca v Lasker 1921, or Capablanca v Alekhine 1927?

CLOSE ENCOUNTERS: PREVIOUS GAMES BETWEEN KORCHNOI AND KARPOV

Karpov and Korchnoi have played 35 serious games against each other, and also one game in a simultaneous display, given by Korchnoi when Karpov was 11 years old. Their full results are given below in tabular form:

Year	Event	Karpov	Korchnoi
1962	Simultaneous Display	½	½
1970	38th USSR Championship	0	1
1971	Training Match	+2=2-2	+2=2-2
1971	Alekhine Memorial	1	0
1971/2	Hastings	0	1
1973	Interzonal	½	½
1973	41st USSR Championship	1	0
1974	Candidates' Final	+3=19-2	+2=19-3

The complete tally is: Karpov 7 wins, Korchnoi 6 wins, and 23 draws.

The little-known training match in 1971 was unusual in that Korchnoi took Black in 5 out of the six games *and forewarned Karpov what opening he was proposing to play.*

Most of the games played since Karpov won his spurs are well known, but the following fairy-tale beginning to the Korchnoi-Karpov relationship is worth reproducing.

Simultaneous Display, Cheliabinsk 1962, Korchnoi — Karpov, Four Knights

1 P-K4 P-K4 2 N-KB3 N-QB3 3 P-Q4 PxP 4 NxP N-B3 5 N-QB3 P-Q3 6 B-QN5 B-Q2 7 0-0 B-K2 8 R-K1 0-0 9 B-B1 R-K1 10 P-KR3 NxN 11 QxN B-B3 12 B-K3 Q-Q2 13 QR-Q1 B-B1 14 B-KN5 B-K2 15 B-B1 P-QR3 16 P-KN4 P-R3 17 P-B4 QR-Q1 18 B-N2 Q-B1 19 Q-Q3 P-QN4 20 P-R3 Q-N2 21 Q-B3 B-B1 22 P-KR4 P-QR4 23 P-N5 PxP 24 RPxP N-R2 25 B-R3 P-Q4 26 PxP RxR+ 27 RxR BxQP 28 NxB QxN 29 QxQ RxQ 30 P-N6 B-B4+ Drawn.

Part II

THE RUN-UP TO THE MATCH

Garlands greeted Viktor Korchnoi and the rest of his party (Petra Leeu-werik, Michael Stean, Yasha Murei and myself) when we arrived in Manila, for the purpose of acclimatisation, two weeks before the start of the match. The whole atmosphere was reminiscent of Disneyland and our spirits were only slightly dampened when the monsoons set in a few days after our arrival.

From Manila we moved in state to Baguio City where Karpov and his entourage had already arrived a few days earlier. Baguio (which means gold in the local language Tagolog) is on North Luxon, an island 150 miles north of Manila, and, being cooler than the main capital, is the summer capital of the Philippines. The City itself is a fortress set in a valley between 5000 ft. mountains and appropriately the organisers had placed the Korchnoi and Karpov parties in separate hotels on mountains on either side of the city so that they could gaze across at each other like the two towers of Minas Ethil and Minas Morgul in Tolkien's *Lord of the Rings*.

Despite reluctance from the Russians to meet the dissident leper Korchnoi more than was necessary, President Marcos insisted on receiving the two players together at the Presidential Palace Malacanung. At the reception he made a statement saying "This match will focus attention on the Philippines especially after the distorted reporting of the Western Press on this country." Curiously he singled out Leonard Barden for criticism on the grounds that he had claimed that the Philippines lacked funds to stage the match. In fact a number of reports in England had expressed doubts based mainly on the fact that no US network was interested in the TV rights which had been expected to raise £1,000,000.

From my own experience I can testify that no expense or effort was spared in the interest of the complete comfort of the players and their delegations. One small example was that, when I ordered soup at the Philippina Plaza, it arrived in a bowl encased in a moulded block of ice into which flowers had been frozen. An even smaller example was the miniature bed which the diminutive world champion had specially made for him by a local carpenter.

I have already introduced the players themselves in the Introduction and I must now introduce their respective heads of delegation who were to play such an important role in the various squabbles which arose both before and during the match.

The Russian leader was one V.D. Baturinsky, a retired colonel — not however the sort of retired colonel who writes to the *London Daily Telegraph*, since his commission was in the KGB. There was no love lost between him and the Korchnoi camp since he was one of the soviet chess bureaucrats who had contributed to Korchnoi's decision to leave the USSR. Korchnoi had clashed with him since, when he led the USSR delegations in the Candidate's matches. At his press conference Korchnoi said Baturinsky should be hung, drawn and quartered for his role as a political prosecutor during the Stalin era.

Baturinsky was confronted by Ms. Petra Leeuwerik. She had previously had little interest in chess when she met Korchnoi in Holland a few months after his defection. But they soon found that the coincidence of their views on communists was more than enough to forge a bond between them and she has been a loyal champion of Korchnoi ever since. Her own reasons for remaining cheerless in the company of Russians are substantial enough. When she was nineteen she was kidnapped from the Russian zone of Vienna on the pretext of being a spy and spent ten years in the notorious Vorkuta concentration camp. She is a stimulating and entertaining person and in view of her history it is hard to blame her for her fierce hatred of the Russians. But even before the match I was worried that she would prove *plus royaliste que le roi* and fan Korchnoi's already fiery disposition. As the match progressed my worries were unfortunately proved to be justified.

After settling in, the two contestants were confronted by the press. Karpov, dressed in a barong with the championship logo topped by a crown embroidered on it, was serene but rather dull and he avoided political questions. In particular he declined to comment on Korchnoi's request that his family be allowed out of the USSR on the grounds that this issue was nothing to do with chess. Asked by Petra Leeuwerik to comment on the fact that his chess autobiography *'Chess is My Life'* bore the same title as Korchnoi's, published a few months earlier, he replied that the title was his publishers' choice. He was, however, provoked into commenting on Korchnoi: "He is a fighter in the full meaning of the word. His play and method are good. He is a very strong chess player but as to his character, I do not appreciate it highly." On the issue of the result of the match, after being told of Korchnoi's confidence in winning he replied, "Maybe Karpov is as sure of victory as he was three years ago. Then I was sure I'd win as I am now." However he declined to make any predictions on the length of the match. "It is very difficult," he said.

Not surprisingly, Korchnoi was more forthcoming. He objected to the size of the Soviet delegation of 16 which included not only strong chess players such as the ex-world champion Tal (officially designated a journalist) and grandmaster Balashov but also, he alleged, "a medician, a PT expert, a psychologist or psychiatrist, a chemistry expert (!), an expert to conduct physical tests during the match and two members of the KGB secret police."

Korchnoi used the quaint word "medician" to mean simply a doctor. But one journalist missheard him and reported that he had said "magician". The report spread rapidly and it is an interesting reflection on the atmosphere surrounding the match that nobody seemed to regard the suggestion of black magic as implausible!

The issue of the size of Karpov's delegation simmered on after the press conference. Petra Leeuwerik, as head of the Korchnoi delegation, demanded that the names and functions of all 16 be disclosed. "It is impossible," she argued, "for them to come here without specific functions since the category of tourist does not exist for Soviet travellers." Baturinsky declined to supply the information on the grounds that the rules of the match did not compel him to do so and his contention was upheld by the Philippino organiser of the match, Campomanes.

Returning to the press conference, Korchnoi said that his life would be in danger from Soviet agents if he damaged Soviet prestige by beating the champion. It was generally considered that this fear was rather far fetched but I was still relieved that I was not invited to act as Korchnoi's food taster!

The centrepiece of Korchnoi's conference was his announcement that he had written an open letter to Chairman Brezhnev demanding that his wife and son should be allowed out of the USSR, thus emulating Martina Navratilova in using his position in the limelight to publicise a private grievance. He denied that Karpov could disclaim responsibility for the acts of a government he supports and called him "one of the jailers of my family". The letter concluded:

"I appeal to you to demonstrate the goodwill necessary for the fulfillment of the conditions of the Helsinki International Agreement, which prescribes the reunification of divided families.

"I invoke your mercy, Mr. Chairman; I beg you to show compassion for two citizens af the USSR, whose life, by decree of fate, is no longer bound to the life of Soviet society. Permit them to leave the Soviet Union."

A copy of this letter was sent to the Russian ambassador to the Philippines. Forewarned of its contents, he returned it unopened.

Korchnoi was only persuaded to speak briefly about the match itself. He said the chances were 50-50 and predicted the contest would be over in 20 games. He castigated the new rule that Karpov should be entitled to a re-match if he lost and left the audience in doubt whether he would abide by this rule if the case arose.

No report of a chess match seems complete these days without a paragraph on death rays, so here goes . . . Petra Leeuwerik prophylactically announced that Korchnoi had brought an anti-ray device with him. Baturinsky retaliated by demanding that Korchnoi's special chair, an olive-green stoll giroflex type costing £700, should be x-rayed but all that was found by an incredulous radiographer was foam rubber.

But the main pre-match dispute concerned which flag Korchnoi should play under. He wanted the Swiss flag on the grounds that he has now resided in Wohlen, Switzerland, for almost a year and proposes to make Switzerland his home and play for the Swiss in the Olympics. He had applied for Swiss nationality and had a letter from the Swiss government consenting to the use of their flag. But all this was not good enough for the Soviets who wanted him to play under a plain white flag with the word *'stateless'* on it. They rejected his counter-proposal that he would play under the hammer and sickle provided that the words 'I've escaped' appeared on it. The dispute dragged on perilously close to the scheduled start of the match and was not resolved until two days before the match was due to start. In the end, after two critical meetings at one of which Baturinsky stormed out bellowing threats to cancel the match unless he got his own way, what Korchnoi called "the diplomacy of the fist", triumphed. Despite the last-minute arrival of an independent legal opinion from Professor Karl Doehring of Heidelberg University, which supported Korchnoi, the jury voted against the Swiss flag. Eventually on the proposal of Colonel Edmondson (USA) a compromise was reached. The Soviet flag would be displayed on the stage but neither player would have a flag on the chess table.

The match now being on again preparations were made for the opening ceremony on 17th July. It was arranged that the Soviet national anthem would be played for Karpov while Korchnoi chose part of the last movement of Beethoven's Ninth symphony, which features the 'Ode to Joy' which Schiller had originally entitled *'Freiheit'* (Liberty) until the censors intervened. This was a case of pseudo-military kitsch in competition with great classical music. Korchnoi had intended to sit down ostentatiously during the Russian national anthem but this gesture proved unnecessary because the orchestra got their music mixed up and played instead the Internationale, which Stalin had dropped as the Soviet National Anthem in 1943. This produced scowls from the Soviets and guffaws from the Korchnoi camp.

The whole chess world was now anxiously waiting for the start of the match.

GAME ONE

After all the preliminary alarms and excursions the stage now seemed set for the first game — but there was one final hiccup. Although both players had previously settled and approved the chess pieces to be used in the match, they both decided at the last minute (finally agreeing on something) that they were too light-weight. Thus a match which had been planned months in advance was in danger of failing to start on time because no suitable chess set was available. Happily, as in 1972, the situation was saved by a *deus ex machina*, cunningly disguised as a human millionaire. But, whereas Jim Slater had to fork out £50,000 to save the Fischer-Spassky match, all that was required of our new hero, Manila magnate Manuel Zamora (may his tribe increase!) was one heavy chess set. This was rushed 150 miles from Manila over tortuous mountain roads and arrived with 15 minutes to spare — 14 minutes too early for full dramatic effect.

The first game itself was an anti-climax. President (Prexy in the local language, Tagolog) Marcos was watching but this did not spur the players to great efforts and after minor inaccuracies on each side the game burnt out to an early draw.

White: Korchnoi
Black: Karpov

Queen's Gambit Declined

1 P-QB4	N-KB3
2 N-QB3	P-K3
3 N-B3	P-Q4
4 P-Q4	B-K2
5 B-N5	P-KR3
6 B-R4	0-0
7 P-K3	P-QN3
8 R-B1	B-N2
9 B-Q3	PxP(?)

9...P-B4 is correct.

10 BxP	QN-Q2
11 0-0	P-B4

12 PxP(?)

12 Q-K2 is a better attempt to retain White's opening advantage, e.g. 12...N-K5 13 NxN BxB 14 N-B3 B-KB3 15 KR-Q1 Q-K2 16 B-R6 QR-N1 17 BxB RxB 18 N-K4 with a plus (Alekhine - Bogoljubow, Mannheim 1937). Alekhine recommended 12...P-R3 13 KR-Q1 P-QN4 as an improvement but White can retain a slight advantage by playing 13 P-R4.

12 . . .	NxP
13 Q-K2	P-R3
14 KR-Q1	Q-K1
15 P-QR3	KN-K5

16 NxN	NxN
17 BxB	QxB
18 N-Q4	KR-B1

DIAGRAM

Draw agreed on Karpov's proposal. The position is lifeless. (Times: 0.52 – 0.52)

GAME TWO

Although countless chess fans all over the world would have been delighted to watch the match, draws and all, if only they could have afforded the fare to the Philippines, in Baguio itself interest temporarily plummetted after the boring first game. The price of tickets was reduced but still the playing hall was almost empty and it proved necessary to enlist a troop of local military cadets to swell the audience.

The second game, although also drawn, was considerably more interesting than the first and featured some splendid theoretical preparation by Korchnoi which extended up to move 24! Korchnoi surprised everyone by shelving the French in favour of the Open Ruy Lopez. Karpov reached an ending with the nominal advantage of bishop for knight but he could make nothing of it and the game was drawn in 29 moves. At the close of the game Korchnoi said "Karpov heard somewhere that bishop was better than knight — in Leonid Stein's hands maybe, but not in his!"

The game was encouraging for the Korchnoi camp, partly because we maintain Karpov plays less well in open positions and partly because Karpov was always behind on the clock - at one point he had used 50 minutes against Korchnoi's 4 minutes.

White: Karpov
Black: Korchnoi

Ruy Lopez

1 P-K4	P-K4
2 N-KB3	N-QB3
3 B-N5	P-QR3
4 B-R4	N-B3
5 0-0	NxP
6 P-Q4	P-QN4
7 B-N3	P-Q4
8 PxP	B-K3
9 P-B3	B-QB4
10 QN-Q2	0-0
11 B-B2	B-B4
12 N-N3	B-KN5

13 NxB	NxN
14 R-K1	

This position is well known to Karpov — see for example his

37

games against Smyslov at Leningrad 1977 and Tilburg 1977 and against Belyavsky at Leningrad 1977. But now Korchnoi produced a new move which clearly caught Karpov unawares.

14 ...	P-Q5
15 P-KR3	B-R4
16 PxP	BxN
17 QxB	NxQP
18 Q-B3	Q-Q4
19 B-K3	NxB
20 QxN(B2)	N-Q6
21 KR-Q1	KR-Q1
22 QxP	

22 QR-B1 may be a little better.

22 ...	QxKP
23 QxQ	NxQ
24 P-QN3	P-B3

25 B-N6	RxR+
26 RxR	R-QB1
27 R-Q2	P-KR4
28 B-K3	K-B2
29 P-B4	

Draw agreed
(Times: 1.55 — 1.35)

GAME THREE

During the second game a yoghurt was delivered to Karpov and nobody appeared to take any notice but when the same thing happened in game 3 the audience burst out laughing — for by now the Great Yoghurt Controversy, for which the match may be remembered long after the chess has been forgotten, was in full swing.

After the second game the Korchnoi camp, in an attempt to ease the tension and parody some of the earlier protests, issued a formal protest claiming that the delivery of a yoghurt could convey a kind of coded message. "Thus a yoghurt after move 20 could signify 'we instruct you to offer a draw'; or a sliced mango could mean 'we order you to decline a draw'. A dish of marinated quails eggs could mean 'play N-N5 at once' and so on. The possibilities are limitless."

Predictably only Baturinsky and Ms. Leeuwerik appeared to take the protest seriously but their intransigence was sufficient to blow the dispute up out of all proportion. After a long meeting of the jury had failed to solve the problem, Lothar Schmid finally saved the day by decreeing that Karpov could have his yoghurt provided that he had only the violet coloured variety served at a fixed time by a designated waiter.

The Great Yoghurt Controversy gave the press a field day and Ian Ward must have enjoyed himself when commenting in *The London Daily Telegraph* on the compromise: "But will the yoghurt crisis now really subside? Herr Schmid is the first to admit the tenuousness of the situation. He fully realises that yoghurt can come in many colours — green, blue, pink, yellow, to name but a few. Under the Schmid ruling a change in the colour of the yoghurt passed to Karpov throws the whole compromise into confusion: for then the Russians must seek official permission once again. 'If it is a violet yoghurt again no mention need be made in advance to me or to the deputy arbiters. In case Mr. Karpov wishes to change beverages, please let an arbiter know in advance of the game by describing the new beverage in a short note.' And in this rarified atmosphere that only chess grandmasters appear to comprehend fully, it appears that there might be serious complications if Herr Schmid is asked to distinguish between, say, mauve and violet yoghurt. The implications remain frightening."

The third game was by far the sharpest of those to date. Korchnoi allowed the Nimzo-Indian Defence for the very first time in all his games against Karpov and achieved an opening advantage using a line he had analysed with Furman in 1967! Furman, ironically, later became Karpov's trainer, and his death earlier this year deprived Karpov of a valuable friend and supporter.

Korchnoi rapidly built up a dominating position, and for most of the game the assembled experts (Najdorf, Byrne, Tal, Euwe etc.) believed he would win with a crushing king-side assault. Korchnoi also held a time advantage of half an hour until the latter stages of the game. However, Korchnoi faltered on move 24 and Karpov was allowed to wriggle out with a draw. White has nothing better at the end.

White: Korchnoi
Black: Karpov

Nimzo-Indian Defence

1 P-QB4	N-KB3
2 P-Q4	P-K3
3 N-QB3	B-N5
4 P-K3	P-B4
5 N-K2	

Rubinstein's move, which avoids doubled pawns. It is the best antidote to the popular Hubner variation (5 B-Q3 N-B3 6 N-B3 BxN+ 7 PxB —Q3) which Black is trying to introduce with his fourth move.

5 . . .	PxP
6 PxP	P-Q4
7 P-B5	N-K5
8 B-Q2	NxB
9 QxN	P-QR4

I believe this is a new move for published theory, although Korchnoi had analysed it privately with Furman. Karpov played 9... P-QR4 very quickly, but he soon slowed down.

Previous tries by Black in this position have been:
(A) 9...P-QN3 10 P-QR3 BxN+ 11 NxB PxP 12 PxP P-QR4 13 B-N5 B-Q2 14 R-B1 P-R5 with approximate equality in Averbakh

-Panno, Portoroz Interzonal 1958. (B) 9...N-B3 10 P-QR3 B-R4 11 P-QN4 B-B2 12 P-N3 P-QN3 13 B-N2 PxP 14 QPxP R-QN1 15 R-QN1 0-0 16 0-0 (16 P-B4!?) 16...B-K4 17 KR-Q1 with a small plus in Korchnoi-Spassky, USSR Championship 1973.

10 P-QR3	BxN
11 NxB	B-Q2
12 B-Q3	P-R5

Here is the point of Black's ninth move. He lames White's queenside pawns, but at the cost of development tempi which White invests to inaugurate a kingside attack.

13 0-0	0-0
14 P-B4	

According to Korchnoi White could also maintain a small plus by operating on the queenside, e.g. 14 QR-B1 P-QN3 15 N-N5 etc. The text is more violent and more creative.

14 . . .	P-KN3
15 K-R1	N-B3
16 B-B2	N-K2

Black rushes one reserve to the defence of his threatened kingside.

17 QR-K1	P-N3
18 R-B3	

White's whole game plan revolves around pushing through the

advance P-KB5, but if Black prevents this with the blockade move ...P-KB4 he will suffer from a weak king pawn and a restricted queen bishop hemmed in by its own pawns.

18 ...   **R-K1?**

Black should have played 18... PxP 19 PxP P-B3! setting up a barrier around his king.

19 R(3)-K3!

A very fine and deep attacking conception, the point of which should be to force through P-KB5.

19 ...   **B-B3**
20 PxP   **QxP**

21 P-KN4

White could strike at once with the combinational blow 21 P-B5 with the following variations:

A) 21...NxP 22 BxN KPxB 23 NxQP! Q-Q1 24 RxR+ BxR 25 RxB+ QxR 26 N-B6+ and wins.
B) 21...NPxP 22 R-N3+ N-N3 23 P-R4 Q-Q1 24 P-R5 Q-R5+ 25 R-R3 Q-B5 26 R(1)-K3 winning.
C) 21... NPxP 22 R-N3+ N-N3 23 P-R4 Q-B2 24 N-K2! B-N4 25 N-B4 K-R1 (If 25...Q-Q1 26 N-R5 QxP+ 27 R-R3 Q-K2 28 Q-R6 P-B3 29 RxP! wins) 26 N-R5 Q-Q1 (Or 26...Q-R4 27 Q-N5! QxP+ 28 K-R2 when the threat of Q-B6+ wins for White, or 26...

R-KN1 27 Q-N5 Q-Q1 28 N-B6 with the lethal P-R5 coming.) 27 Q-R6 QxP+ 28 R-R3 QxR(K8)+ 29 K-R2 R-KN1 30 N-B6 R-N2 31 QxPch RxQ 32 RxR mate. The geometry of the two variations with the rook sacrifice on K1 is striking (Q-R4xR+ or Q-KR5x R+). However, Black has a big improvement after 26...P-B3! 27 RxN PxR 28 Q-R6+ Q-R2 29 QxQ+ KxQ 30 NxP+ K-N2 31 NxR+ RxN 32 R-K3 when White has only a slightly better ending.

21 ...   **Q-B2**
22 P-B5

If 22 R-R3 Black can hold on by 22...Q-Q3! 23 P-B5 KPxP 24 Q-R6 Q-B3! but not, however, 22...K-N2 23 P-B5 N-N1 24 P-B6+ NxP 25 Q-R6+ K-N1 26 R-KB1 Q-K2 27 P-N5 N-R4 28 RxN PxR 29 QxP+ K-R1 30 Q-R8 mate.

22 ...   **KPxP**
23 PxP   **Q-Q3**
24 R-R3?

Optically impressive but it allows a draw. White can maintain the pressure with 24 R-K5! Q-B3 25 Q-R6 when he still has a strong attack. Another promising idea is 24 R-N3 with slow build up of pressure on the Black king.

24 ...   **NxP**
25 BxN   **PxB**
26 R-N1+   **K-R1**
27 R-R6   **R-K3**
28 RxR   **QxR!**

Not 28...PxR 29 Q-N5 Q-B1 30 N-K2 followed by N-B4 with advantage to White in spite of his pawn minus, e.g. 30...P-K4 31 N-N3 PxP 32 NxP P-Q6 33 N-Q4!

29 Q-N5   **Q-N3**
30 Q-R4   **Q-K3**

Draw agreed
White has nothing better than repetition of the position.
(Times: 2.33 − 2.17)

GAME FOUR

25th July

While the Great Yoghurt Controversy was rumbling on, Karpov created a minor diversion by complaining that his chair was too low. A cushion was supplied but Karpov complained this made the chair too high and so a duplicate of the original chair, brought over from Manila, was specially modified to make it four centimetres higher. But Karpov rejected this too and finally plumped for the original chair with a smaller cushion. The Little Russian Bear was now satisfied.

In the fourth game Korchnoi varied from game 2 on move 14 and Karpov, although sitting comfortably, could gain absolutely no advantage, conceding a draw by repetition on move 19. Such a game is caviar to the general and some non-chess playing journalists were going berserk with frustration, dubbing Baguio "a land based ship of fools". There were fears that if it carried on raining we would not be land based much longer. Nevertheless, game 4 was of great theoretical importance, fitting in with Korchnoi's overall match strategy of nullifying Karpov's White openings, comparable to neutralising the serve in tennis.

White: Karpov
Black: Korchnoi

Ruy Lopez

1 P-K4	P-K4
2 N-KB3	N-QB3
3 B-N5	P-QR3
4 B-R4	N-B3
5 0-0	NxP
6 P-Q4	P-QN4
7 B-N3	P-Q4
8 PxP	B-K3
9 P-B3	B-QB4
10 QN-Q2	0-0
11 B-B2	B-B4
12 N-N3	B-KN5
13 NxB	NxN
14 R-K1	

All so far as in the second game where Black played 14...P-Q5.

14 . . .   B-R4

A surprise as Korchnoi himself in Volume C of the *Encyclopedia of Chess Openings* published in 1974 claims this move to be a blunder losing to 15 B-N5 BxN (or 15... Q-Q2 16 B-K3 N-K3 17 BxP+!) 16 QxB QxB 17 QxQP (Bronstein-Flohr, USSR 1944). However, since then he had discovered that Black can equalise by 17...QR-K1! Karpov now thought for 40 minutes but was unable to find any way of obtaining the advantage.

15 P-KR3   R-K1

16 B-B4	N-K3
17 B-Q2	N-B4
18 B-B4	N-K3
19 B-Q2	

DIAGRAM

Draw agreed
(Times: 0.50 − 0.41)

GAME FIVE

After the uneventful fourth game the audience were desperate for some real action and they were not disappointed. The fifth game proved to be one of the most dramatic ever played in a world championship match.

After Karpov had rashly tried to exploit his time trouble by playing a very loosening move, Korchnoi adjourned in an apparently won position. The following morning there was a small breakfast party to celebrate the second anniversary of Korchnoi's defection. The centrepiece was a birthday cake, supplied by the Pines Hotel, decorated with a knight, two candles and the words "Happy Birthday Viktor Korchnoi — Good Luck". Asked if he wanted any special present, Korchnoi answered "It's not difficult to guess".

But after the ball was over Korchnoi arrived at the battlefield to find that Karpov had sealed an unexpected cavalry manoeuvre. However, he kept his head while Karpov did his best to lose his. But alas, just when Napoleon should have met his Waterloo, the Duke of Wellington fell off his horse and the battle was again evenly poised. Further inaccuracies allowed Korchnoi to adjourn a second time in a favourable position, but this time no win could be found. Korchnoi nonetheless resumed the game and made Karpov demonstrate that he knew how to draw. Eventually Korchnoi was satisfied and delivered stalemate on move 124.

The game set two records. It was the longest ever world championship game, breaking the record previously held by the fourteenth game of the 1961 Tal-Botvinnik match, and the first ever to end in stalemate.

White: Korchnoi
Black: Karpov

Nimzo-Indian Defence

1 P-QB4	N-KB3
2 P-Q4	P-K3
3 N-QB3	B-N5
4 P-K3	P-B4
5 N-K2	P-Q4

Varying from 5...PxP with which he failed to equalise in the third game.

6 P-QR3	BxN+
7 NxB	BPxP
8 KPxP	PxP
9 BxP	N-B3
10 B-K3	0-0
11 0-0	P-QN3
12 Q-Q3	

More pointed is 12 Q-B3 B-N2 13 B-Q3 according to our analysis after the game. The text follows ancient precedent, but against Karpov's accurate defence it promises very little.

| 12 ... | B-N2 |
| 13 QR-Q1 | P-KR3 |

Improving on Botvinnik-Tolush, USSR 1965, where Black played 13 . . . N-K2 which allowed 14 B-KN5.

14 P-B3!

A new move which prepares a highly original kingside pawn storm. The move was unexpected and, according to Korchnoi, Karpov now began to dislike the position although objectively Black stands quite well. Further points of 14 P-B3 are to blunt the power of Black's QB and to prepare a new avenue for White's own QB.

14 ...	N-K2
15 B-B2	N(B3)-Q4
16 B-R2	N-B5
17 Q-Q2	N(B5)-N3

The point of this artificial manoeuvre was to deprive White's QB of his KR4 square but White achieves this anyway by a thrust of his KRP.

18 B-N1	Q-Q2
19 P-KR4	KR-Q1
20 P-R5	N-KB1
21 B-R4	P-B3

Intended to limit the scope of White's bishop but now the weakness of Black's KP becomes significant.

| 22 N-K4 | N-Q4 |

DIAGRAM

23 P-KN4

Not everyone would have the courage to play such a move. There is an ever-present danger that White may become severely

overextended. Opinions were divided as to who stood better. Najdorf favoured White, Stean preferred Black, and I had no idea at all. A typically difficult 'Korchnoi position' has in fact now arisen. The press rooms were in the cellars beneath the auditorium, and much excitement was generated at the Byrne-Najdorf 'Experts Table'.

23 ...	QR-B1
24 B-N3	B-R3
25 KR-K1	R-B3
26 R-QB1	N-K2
27 RxR	QxR

This looks careless. After 27... NxR 28 N-Q6 I believe the position is still in equilibrium. The move played loses tempi.

| 28 B-QR2 | Q-Q2 |
| 29 N-Q6 | B-N2 |

Now White gains the permanent advantage of the two bishops, but if Black challenges the knight by 29...N-B1? 30 RxP! NxR 31 Q-K3 is a winning sacrifice.

30 NxB	QxN
31 Q-K3	K-R1
32 R-QB1	N-Q4
33 Q-K4	Q-Q2
34 B-N1	Q-N4
35 P-N4	Q-Q2

A retreat, but if Black plays

incautiously 35...P-R4 36 B-Q6!
RxB 37 R-B8 K-N1 Q-R7+
etc. wins.

| 36 Q-Q3 | Q-K2 |
| 37 K-B2 | P-B4? |

Typical Karpov. With Korchnoi
in time trouble he plays 'va-
banque' instead of going for the
objectively best defence. It is of
course extra risky to break the
position open when White has the
two bishops.

38 PxP	PxP
39 R-K1	Q-B3
40 B-K5	Q-R5+
41 B-N3	Q-B3
42 R-R1	

We all thought this ingenious
move would win. Karpov now
spent nineteen minutes sealing.

| 42 . . . | N-R2! |

A brilliant move which gives
Black tremendous counterchances,
in spite of the loss of a pawn.
Curiously, the whole defensive
concept behind Black's move was
entirely overlooked by grandmasters Byrne and Najdorf and, I
hate to admit, by Korchnoi's
whole group (including Korchnoi
himself) despite one whole night
of analysis. A case of mass hypno-
tism??? This was in fact the first
game where Zukhar was noticed

in the audience trying to stare
Korchnoi down.

43 B-K5	Q-N4
44 QxP	Q-Q7+
45 K-N3	N(2)-B3

The intention becomes clear.
The knights support each other,
and White faces extreme danger
from the devastation which
surrounds his own king. Korchnoi
played the next few moves superbly (without the aid of adjournment analysis) but he got into
raging time trouble finding them.

| 46 R-N1 | R-K1 |
| 47 B-K4! | |

It seems that this stroke escaped
the Soviet analysts, since Karpov
now spent fifty minutes on his
reply. White cannot play the
apparently logical 47 K-R3 in
view of 47...RxB followed by
...N-B5+ and White is crushed.

47 . . .	N-K2
48 Q-R3	R-QB1
49 K-R4	

A unique method of clearing the
KN-file, but Korchnoi, now on
top again, only had a couple of
minutes for seven moves. Faced
with this predicament Karpov
tried to solve his problems by
blitzing Korchnoi, but during the
blitz he himself played some
extremely weak moves.

| 49 . . . | R-B8 |
| 50 Q-N3 | |

50 Q-N2, forcing exchanges, is
more clearcut.

| 50 . . . | RxR |

If 50...Q-N4+ 51 QxQ PxQ+ 52
RxP R-R8+ 53 K-N3 R-N8+ 54
K-B4 N(3)-Q4+ 55 BxN NxB+
56 K-B5 N-K2+ 57 K-K6 RxR 58
KxN RxP 59 P-B4 followed by
P-Q5, P-Q6 etc. winning.

51 QxR	K-N1

Beginning an insane king march.

52 Q-N3	K-B2?
53 B-N6+	K-K3?

The foolhardy king continues his march to the scaffold, but fortunately the hangman is asleep.

54 Q-R3+	K-Q4

55 B-K4+??

With only two moves to go to the time control Korchnoi throws his whole advantage away by one of the worst blunders in world championship history, ranking with Tchigorin's horrendous oversight in the last game of his second match with Steinitz. Of course, 55 B-B7+ followed by 56 Q-K6+ wins easily.

55 . . .	NxB
56 PxN+	KxP
57 Q-N4+	K-Q6
58 Q-B3+	

The calm has descended after the storm. Korchnoi thought forty minutes over this move in a desperate attempt to find winning chances but to no real avail. He has a slight advantage due to the weakness of Black's pawn on KN2 but it is virtually certain that the 'wrong-coloured rook's pawn' will eventually play a decisive role.

58 . . .	Q-K6

59 K-N4	QxQ+
60 KxQ	P-N3?

This makes Black's defensive task more difficult and gives Korchnoi new hope. 60..K-N4 draws easily. Perhaps Karpov couldn't believe he was still on the board and found it hard to concentrate.

61 B-Q6	N-B4
62 K-B4	

Karpov had apparently overlooked this move. If now 62... NxB 63 PxP N-K1 64 K-K5 followed by 65 P-Q5 and Black cannot prevent one of the two White passed pawns queening. Now he has to sacrifice his knight but the position is still just tenable.

62 . . .	N-R5
63 K-N4	PxP+
64 KxN	KxP
65 B-N8	P-R4
66 B-Q6	K-B5
67 KxP	P-R5
68 KxP	K-N6
69 P-N5	K-B5
70 K-N5	KxP

As White's bishop does not control his RP's queening square his only chances of winning lie in either capturing both Black pawns while the Black king is too far away from the queening square or stalemating the black king temporarily and so forcing Black to play ...P-N5 when White's rook's pawn is converted to a winning knight's pawn. But Karpov defends perfectly and neither eventually occurrs.

71 K-B5	K-R3
72 K-K6	K-R2
73 K-Q7	K-N2
74 B-K7	K-R2

75 K-B7	K-R1
76 B-Q6	K-R2
77 K-B8	K-R3
78 K-N8	P-N4
79 B-N4	K-N3
80 K-B8	K-B3
81 K-Q8	K-Q4
82 K-K7	K-K4
83 K-B7	K-Q4
84 K-B6	K-Q5
85 K-K6	K-K5
86 B-B8	K-Q5
87 K-Q6	K-K5
88 B-N7	K-B5
89 K-K6	K-B6
90 K-K5	K-N5
91 B-B6	K-R4

Here the game was adjourned a second time. Korchnoi has made no progress in the last twenty moves but now had a chance to consult reference books and analyse the position thoroughly. I telexed Bob Wade to consult his Library in London but no win was to be found. Our own ending books had been lost with Murei's luggage in Tel Aviv, but miraculously they arrived on the morning the game was to be resumed. Alas they merely confirmed the position was a draw.

92 K-B5	K-R3

93 B-Q4	K-R2
94 K-B6	K-R3
95 B-K3+	K-R4
96 K-B5	K-R5
97 B-Q2	K-N6
98 B-N5	K-B6
99 B-B4	K-N7

The only move! One typical way to lose is 99...K-B7 100 K-K4 K-K7 101 B-N8 K-B7 102 K-Q5 K-B6 103 K-B5 K-K5 104 KxP K-Q4 105 B-R2 K-K3 106 KxP K-Q2 107 K-N5 K-B1 108 K-B6 and Black's king is cut off. The existence of such pitfalls for Black show that Korchnoi's playing on so long in a theoretically drawn position was not just bloody-mindedness.

100 B-Q6	K-B6
101 B-R2	K-N7
102 B-B7	K-B6
103 B-Q6	K-K6
104 K-K5	K-B6
105 K-Q5	K-N5
106 K-B5	K-B4
107 KxP	K-K3
108 K-B6	K-B3
109 K-Q7	K-B2
110 B-K7	K-N1
111 K-K6	K-N2
112 B-B5	K-N1
113 K-B6	K-R2
114 K-B7	K-R1
115 B-Q4+	K-R2
116 B-N2	K-R3
117 K-N8	K-N3
118 B-N7	K-B4
119 K-B7	K-N4
120 B-N2	K-R3
121 B-B1+	K-R2
122 B-Q2	K-R1
123 B-B3+	K-R2
124 B-N7 stalemate	

(Times: 6-02 — 6.01 — a moral victory for Karpov?)

GAME SIX

29th July

The sixth game was played in the interval between the second and third sessions of the fifth game. Many people were surprised that neither player exercised his right to postpone the game after their traumatic experiences in the previous encounter. No doubt each player would have been delighted if the other had chosen to postpone but neither wished to waste one of his ration of three postponements.

As it was the game cannot have taken much out of the players, as it was drawn in 23 moves. Korchnoi stood slightly better in the final position and in normal circumstances would probably have played on.

Karpov switched from 1 P-K4 to the English Opening, but again obtained no advantage with White. It was suggested that Karpov was deliberately soft pedalling with White in order to discover Korchnoi's main line defences and thus prepare more deeply for them at a later stage. If this policy was deliberate it certainly exposed him to a rough time with Black and at this stage in the match he was observed to be looking tired and haggard.

White: Karpov
Black: Korchnoi

English Opening

1 P-QB4	P-K4
2 N-QB3	N-KB3
3 N-B3	N-B3
4 P-KN3	B-N5
5 B-N2	0-0
6 0-0	P-K5
7 N-K1	BxN
8 QPxB	P-KR3
9 N-B2	R-K1

So far we have been following the ninth game of the 1974 match. In that game Karpov was Black and play continued 9...P-QN3 10 B-K3 B-N2 11 N-Q5 N-K4. In the present game Korchnoi varies by developing his QB on KB4 and overprotecting his KP à la Nimzo-witsch.

10 N-K3	P-Q3
11 Q-B2	P-QR4
12 P-QR4	Q-K2
13 N-Q5	

If 13 P-B4 PxP e.p. 14 PxP Q-K4 15 B-Q2 Q-QB4 16 QR-K1 B-K3 17 P-N3 P-Q4 Black has some initiative as the White knight on K3 hinders the co-ordination of his pieces.

13 . . .	NxN
14 PxN	N-N1
15 B-K3	B-B4
16 P-R3	N-Q2

17 P-QB4	P-QN3
18 Q-B3	N-B4
19 P-N3	Q-Q2
20 K-R2	R-K2
21 B-Q4	P-KB3
22 QR-B1	Q-K1
23 Q-K3	

DIAGRAM

Draw agreed

Black stands better and should have declined the draw, e.g. 23... Q-R4 24 R-B3 B-N5 25 R-K1 QR-K1 with the threat of 26... N-Q6 27 PxN PxP 28 QxR RxQ 29 RxR P-Q7 winning.

(Times: 1.25 — 1.05)

GAME SEVEN

1st and 2nd August

The seventh game provided high drama, but still no result. Korchnoi
played the first half of the game superbly. He produced an opening
innovation as early as move six and Karpov was soon forced to sacrifice
the exchange for inadequate compensation. But the position remained
very complex and gradually Korchnoi ran short of time. His position
steadily deteriorated and when the game was adjourned he was faced by
two connected passed pawns on the sixth rank which seemed certain to
decide the game after a few spite checks. Nobody at that stage doubted
that Karpov was about to register the first win and Baturinsky triumph-
antly heralded the victory on Philippino television that evening.

We started analysing the adjourned position in a state of deep
depression but it gradually became clear that Korchnoi could fight on.
The key defensive resource was found by Murei, appropriately enough on
his thirty-eighth birthday. When we finally abandoned analysis at 7 a.m.
we had still not solved the position. We had found neither a clear win for
Karpov nor a clear draw for Korchnoi. To our astonishment Karpov came
to the board next day and offered a draw, which was of course accepted.
As the players were seen signing the score sheets most of the spectators
assumed Korchnoi had resigned and pandemonium broke loose when it
was announced that the game was drawn. "They'll never believe me in
Argentina" lamented Najdorf.

Asian Junior Champion, Murray Chandler, articulated the question in
everyone's mind for New Zealand radio:

"Why was Karpov so sure that Korchnoi had found the crucial saving
continuation? Why did he not even probe to find out just how much
Korchnoi knew? Personally I think Karpov was just plain gutless. He
could have played on and forced Korchnoi to prove he had found a
saving variation. Karpov would not have risked anything."

Is it too devious to suggest that, having decided the position was drawn
and that Korchnoi would almost certainly find the correct defence,
Karpov was trying to mock Korchnoi's action in playing on so long in the
drawn ending in the fifth game?

The seventh game incidentally set a new record for the number of draws
at the start of a world championship match, depriving the 1966 Petrosian
vs. Spassky encounter of that dubious honour. Wags were predicting that
the match would last till Christmas – 1979. More seriously there was

speculation that the World Team Championship, scheduled to begin in mid-October, would be postponed.

White: Korchnoi
Black: Karpov

Nimzo-Indian Defence

1 P-Q4	N-KB3
2 P-QB4	P-K3
3 N-QB3	B-N5
4 P-K3	O-O

Karpov varies from 4...P-B4 with which he got into hot water in the third and fifth games, but Korchnoi still has something up his sleeve.

5 B-Q3	P-B4
6 P-Q5	

An entirely new move suggested by Murei. The idea is either to reach a Benoni-like structure after 6...PxP 7 PxP P-Q3 or else after 6...P-QN4, which Karpov actually plays, to achieve the sort of position in which Karpov does not feel at home. If Black tries 6...PxP 7 PxP NxP 8 BxP+ KxB 9 QxN White has some advantage, due to his central grip and the exposed Black king, for which the bishop pair offers insufficient compensation.

6 ...	P-QN4

After twenty minutes thought Karpov accepts the challenge and plays the most active move. This must have been a difficult decision as he never feels particularly comfortable when he has to offer a gambit.

7 PxKP	BPxP
8 PxP	B-N2
9 N-B3	P-Q4
10 O-O	QN-Q2
11 N-K2	Q-K1

Black certainly has counterplay for his pawn in the shape of a powerful centre, but this move looks too artificial and supports the view that Karpov is not a gambit master.

12 N-N3	P-K4
13 B-B5	P-N3
14 B-R3	P-QR3

If Black tries to prevent White's next move by 14...P-KR3, 15 P-K4 smashes the position open to White's advantage.

15 N-N5!

A very good move which wins the exchange. Although the position is tense, and indeed one of the most original ever to occur in the opening of a World Championship game, there was a general feeling in the press room that White was now on top. Another idea for White is 15 PxP BxP 16 BxN QxB 17 NxP but it looks too risky.

15 ...	PxP
16 N-K6	P-B5
17 B-Q2	B-B4

18 N-B7	Q-K2
19 NxR	RxN
20 P-R3	N-N3
21 Q-B2	B-B1
22 BxB	RxB
23 B-R5	

Also good is the pawn sacrifice 23 B-N4 BxB 24 PxB QxP 25 R-R7 opening lines for the rooks. Korchnoi is one of the greatest exponents in exploiting the advantage of the exchange, but from now on he begins to contradict this image.

23 ...	QN-Q2
24 Q-Q2	B-Q3
25 B-N4	N-B4
26 BxN	BxB
27 K-R1	Q-Q3
28 QR-Q1	

I prefer 28 P-B4 trying to blast open lines at once.

28 ...	K-R1

29 Q-B2
Korchnoi was now losing the thread of the game and drifting into time trouble and so Black begins to get superb compensation. Correct was 29 P-K4 P-Q5 30 Q-N5 N-Q2 31 P-B4 PxP 32 N-K2 followed by NxBP and N-Q5 when White should win.

29 ...	Q-K3
30 N-K2	Q-B3

31 P-R3	R-K1
32 P-QN4??	

Every schoolboy knows you can't play moves like that. Now Black obtains two lusty passed pawns.

32 ...	B-N3
33 Q-N2	K-N1
34 KR-K1	K-B2
35 Q-B2?	

Another lemon which eases the advance of Black's passed pawns.

35 ...	P-Q5
36 N-N3	R-Q1
37 PxP	PxP
38 Q-Q2	P-Q6

38...R-Q2 looks safer but the text is good enough.

39 Q-R6
A desperate attempt to obtain counterplay which is remarkably successful.

39 ...	P-B6
40 N-K4	NxN?

Karpov was now also in time trouble and throws away the win with the last move before the time control. 40...K-N1 leaves White with no counter to the expansion of the passed pawns.

41 QxRP+	K-B1

The famous adjourned position.
42 Q-R8+
The sealed move after which a

draw was **agreed**. Here now is a summary of the analysis which led us to the unexpected conclusion that Black has no clear win:

A) 42 Q-R8+ K-B2 43 Q-R7+ K-B3 44 Q-R4+ K-N2 (or 44... N-N4 45 P-B4 followed by PxN+) 45 RxN R-K1 46 RxR QxR 47 RxP Q-K8+ (or 47...P-B7 48 Q-KB4 Q-K8+ 49 K-R2 P-B8=Q 50 R-Q7+) 48 K-R2 B-B2+ 49 P-N3 QxP+ with a draw since White has the threat of R-Q7+ and if Black takes the rook there is perpetual check.

B) 42 Q-R8+ K-B2 43 Q-R7+ K-K1 44 Q-N8+ K-Q2 45 RxP+ K-B1, 46 RxR+ BxR 47 K-N1! This is Murei's miracle ingredient. Black now has trouble co-ordinating his pieces and the position can become double edged, which is probably what frightened Karpov off, e.g.:

B1) 47...K-Q2 48 P-QR4 PxP 49 P-N5 QxP 50 QxP (Not 50 RxN? Q-N8+) 50...N-Q3 51 Q-N7+ and QxP.

B2) 47...P-N4 48 P-QR4 N-B3 (48...PxP? 49 P-N5) 49 PxP NxQ (49...QxKNP+ only liberates White's king) 50 PxQ N-K2 51 R-R-K5 N-N3 52 R-K2. White then puts his rook on QB2 and leaves it there, even allowing ...NxR KxN with a draw.

B3) 47...N-Q7 (If 47...P-B7 48 R-QB1 plus Q-N3 or Q-R2) 48 R-QB1 Q-B5 (Or 48...P-N4 49 P-KR4 PxP 50 Q-N4+ K-N1 51 Q-N8 etc.) 49 QxP N-K5 (or 49... N-N6 50 Q-B5+ and another check will win the pawn on Black's QB6.) 50 R-B2 Q-Q6 51 RxPch QxR 52 QxN and Black's extra piece cannot win. But if Black wishes to play for a win he can try 50...Q-Q4 when the position remains obscure, but Black cannot stand worse.

(Times: 2.32 — 2.40)

GAME EIGHT

It is well known that Korchnoi plays less well when he is angry and before the eighth game the Soviets pulled off a master stroke which made him see red. Without warning Karpov coyly refused the customary hand-shake at the beginning of the game and Korchnoi was left with his hand suspended pointlessly in mid-air.

Simultaneously, in the press centre beneath the playing hall, the Soviet press chief Roshal issued a rather vague statement justifying Karpov's action: "Recent events have shown that the challenger has not given up his line of intensification of the tension of the situation .... Under such circumstances Mr. Karpov does not wish to shake hands with Mr. Korchnoi."

This immoral, but astute, action by the Russians appeared to throw Korchnoi off balance. Mistaking, according to one commentator, the playing hall for a casino, he played an absurdly risky innovation which formed no part of our prepared analysis. Karpov refuted this with crisp efficiency and finished off with some nice fireworks. After seven indecisive games the business of winning suddenly looked so easy!

After the game Korchnoi relieved his feelings a little by refusing to sign the scoresheet but the following morning he relented and signed.

I stumbled into a hornet's nest by remarking that Karpov's refusal to shake hands would at least save Korchnoi having to go and wash his hands. This provoked the sharp rebuke from Baturinsky that, by associating with the likes of Korchnoi and Ms. Leeuwerik, I had lost "the traits characterising an English gentleman" (whatever they may be). Suitably contrite I withdrew my offending comment and sent Baturinsky a cigar of peace but this was returned (unsmoked!) together with a cake of soap autographed by the great man himself. I haven't had the heart to use it, and it now forms one of my favourite souvenirs of this soap opera.

After the game Karpov celebrated his victory with the laconic comment "At last!". The following day the Terraces Plaza Hotel threw a party for him and, not to be outdone by Korchnoi's earlier 'birthday party' at the Pines Hotel, they provided a cake with one candle on it. I was not invited and unfortunately missed the sight of a beaming Baturinsky dancing in traditional Ifugao garb.

Karpov now led 1-0 with 7 draws.

White: Karpov
Black: Korchnoi

Ruy Lopez

1 P-K4	P-K4
2 N-KB3	N-QB3
3 B-N5	P-QR3
4 B-R4	N-B3
5 0-0	NxP
6 P-Q4	P-QN4
7 B-N3	P-Q4
8 PxP	B-K3
9 QN-Q2	

Varying from 9 P-B3 which was played in the second and fourth games.

9 ...	N-B4
10 P-B3	P-N3

A new provocative and weak move. This unwise innovation was improvised by Korchnoi at the board and formed no part of our preparation. The move is partly motivated by our theory that Karpov does not like to gambit pawns, but the gambit which the text allows is more murderous than speculative.

Despite the weakness of Black's move, Karpov must have been disappointed to be denied the chance to play his innovation 11 N-N5! after the standard move 10...P-Q5. But he was to get his opportunity in his next game with White.

11 Q-K2	B-N2
12 N-Q4	

DIAGRAM

12 ...	NxP?

Consistent but suicidal. Black duly wins a pawn but at the cost of allowing his kingside to be smashed and losing the right to castle — far too high a price.

13 P-B4	N-B5

13...N(K4)-Q6 is a small improvement but it is also not very promising, e.g. 14 P-B5 NxB 15 QRxN PxP 16 NxBP 0-0 17 B-B2 with a fierce attack in prospect.

14 P-B5	PxP
15 NxP	R-KN1

Making the best of a bad job. In some lines Black sneaks some counterplay on the KN file.

16 NxN

A simple solution, quite in Karpov's style, but 16 B-B2 is probably more deadly.

16 ...	QPxN

Korchnoi thought for thirty-five minutes over this move, which showed that something had gone wrong. 16...NPxN was also bad, e.g. 17 B-B2 K-Q2 18 NxB RxN 19 Q-K5 Q-KN1 20 R-B2 P-B3 21 QxKBP R-B2 22 Q-Q4 RxR 23 QxR R-KB1 24 QxN B-R6 25 B-K4 PxB 26 B-N5 and wins. This is only a sample variation but it illustrates the unhappy plight of Black's exposed king.

If instead 16...NxB 17 RPxN PxN 18 PxP PxP 19 B-R6 and Black will be mown down in the centre.

17 B-B2

Best. If 17 NxB+ RxN 18 Q-K5, forking two pieces, 18...RxP+ 19 KxR Q-Q4+ 20 QxQ BxQ+ followed by ...PxB gives Black countplay.

17 . . .   N-Q6?

By now it is just a question of choosing the lesser evil, which would have been 17...Q-Q4 18 B-R6 BxB 19 NxB R-KB1.

18 B-R6!

Korchnoi freely admitted he had overlooked this move.

18 . . .   B-B1?

Two better chances were 18...B-R1 or 18...BxB 19 NxB R-N3 20 NxP Q-K2, though both are fairly forlorn.

19 QR-Q1	Q-Q4
20 BxN	PxB
21 RxP	Q-B3

The original idea was 21...B-B4+ 22 K-R1 RxP 23 QxR QxR

24 QxR+ K-Q2 and Black wins. But now Korchnoi saw that instead 23 RxQ RxQ 24 RxB wins for White.

22 BxB   Q-N3+

If 22...KxB 23 N-Q4 wins a piece.

23 K-R1	KxB
24 Q-B3	

The position now looks like a Muzio King's Gambit where White has not had to sacrifice a piece.

24 . . .	R-K1
25 N-R6	R-N2
26 R-Q7!	

Simple but pleasing. 26...BxR allows 27 QxP+ RxQ 28 RxR mate. The threat is now 27 RxP+ and there is no satisfactory defence.

26 . . .	R-QN1
27 NxP	BxR
28 N-Q8+	Black resigned

(Times 1.58 — 2.25)

GAME NINE

5th August

The spotlight now falls on Dr. Vladimir Zukhar, a noted hypnotist (para-psychologist, necromancer or what you will) who was suspected by Korchnoi of trying to hypnotise him by sitting at the front of the audience and rivetting his gaze onto Korchnoi throughout the games.

He was first recognised by Ms. Leeuwerik during the fifth game. Ever resourceful, she frightened him away by sitting down beside him and offering him a copy of the *Gulag Archipelago*, but he later reappeared on a more distant tuffet and the dispute which was to take over the headlines from the Great Yoghurt Controversy was under way.

As Korchnoi was clearly being disturbed by Zukhar I wrote to Campomanes before the eighth game setting out our objections and asking that Zukhar be seated with the rest of the Soviet delegation at the back of the playing hall. The matter was considered by the jury which resolved that if the Chief Arbiter Schmid considered that Korchnoi was being disturbed he should exercise his powers under match regulation 4.56 which states: "The arbiter shall not permit the players to be unnecessarily disturbed." The dispute lay dormant during the eighth game, when it was overshadowed by the handshaking issue, but at the beginning of the ninth game Ms. Leeuwerik asked Schmid to exercise his powers to have Zukhar removed. Schmid asked Zukhar to join the rest of the Soviet delegation at the back of the hall, but in the end he merely moved from the fifth to the seventh row.

After this coup Ms. Leeuwerik announced proudly "Viktor does not know anything about this because he did not notice him." Later, on her own initiative, she tried to get play moved to a closed room, but Korchnoi was not at that time disturbed by Zukhar and he did not want to move. Ms. Leeuwerik commented angrily and illogically, "Viktor has gone crazy. He doesn't know he is being disturbed." She was obviously unaware of the undertones of self-satire in her remarks.

The ninth game itself followed the pattern which had become all too familiar. Korchnoi obtained the better position as White and converted this to a winning advantage but ran short of time and allowed Karpov to escape with a draw.

So far Korchnoi had obtained won positions in four games, the third (probably), fifth, seventh and ninth, whereas Karpov had only obtained two won positions, in the seventh and eighth games. Yet it was Karpov who was leading the match by one game. On the basis of this contra-dictory evidence opinions were divided as to who was favourite to win the match. Karpov supporters claimed that Korchnoi was likely to run out of steam and that if Korchnoi was already one down before Karpov had played himself into form there could be little hope for him when Karpov really got going. Korchnoi supporters retorted that Karpov was in fact playing to his normal standard and Korchnoi's dynamism was exposing his weaknesses more efficiently than his other recent opponents have been able to achieve. If Korchnoi continued to obtain won positions with such ease he was bound to start winning them eventually. Events in the next few games were to lend suppport to both these views.

Karpov now led 1-0 with 8 draws.

White: Korchnoi
Black: Karpov

Queen's Gambit Declined

1 P-QB4	N-KB3
2 N-QB3	P-K3
3 N-B3	P-Q4
4 P-Q4	B-K2
5 B-B4	0-0
6 P-K3	P-B4
7 QPxP	BxP
8 Q-B2	N-B3
9 R-Q1	Q-R4
10 P-QR3	B-K2
11 N-Q2	P-K4
12 B-N5	P-Q5
13 N-N3	Q-Q1
14 B-K2	

14 . . .   P-KR3?

Better was 14...N-KN5 as played

in Portisch-Spassky, Havanna 1966.

15 BxN	BxB
16 0-0	B-K3
17 N-B5	Q-K2
18 NxB	QxN
19 N-Q5	QR-Q1
20 B-Q3?	

This allows Black to equalise. Correct was 20 P-K4 N-K2 21 B-B3 NxN 22 KPxN followed by P-B5 with a clear advantage since White's passed pawns are the more dangerous. If Black does not swap knights White's mobile pawns (P-QN4/P-B5/B-B4 etc.) are worth more than Black's blockaded passed pawn.

20 . . .	N-K2
21 NxB+	QxN
22 PxP	PxP
23 KR-K1	R-Q2?

A mistake which allows White to secure the only open file. 23... N-N3!, planning to exchange this knight for White's bishop, would have maintained equality.

24 R-K4	N-B3
25 Q-K2	P-KN3
26 R-K1	K-N2
27 P-QN4	P-N3
28 Q-N4!	

Korchnoi cleverly translates his central grip into a kingside attack. But now he only had twenty-five minutes for his next twelve moves.

28 ...	KR-Q1
29 P-KR4	P-KR4
30 Q-N3	

30 Q-N5 keeps Black sewn up positionally but the text is more aggressive.

| 30 ... | Q-Q3 |
| 31 P-B4 | |

Threatening a devastating sacrifice with R-K6!

31 ...	R-K2
32 RxR	NxR
33 R-K5	P-R4!

A good practical decision. When in extreme danger Karpov usually manages to complicate matters and exploit Korchnoi's time-trouble.

34 RxKRP

After the game Korchnoi claimed that 34 PxP PxP 35 RxQRP would win, but the text is also excellent.

| 34 ... | PxP |
| 35 PxP | QxNP |

DIAGRAM

36 R-QN5

A time-trouble reaction, after which Karpov crawls out unscathed. Logical is 36 R-K5!

which recentralises the rook, creates threats of P-B5 and P-R5 and defends White's own hinterland. I believe this wins, e.g. 36 R-K5 N-B3 37 R-K2 Q-B6 38 P-B5 N-N5 39 Q-K5+ K-N1 40 PxP QxB 41 PxP+.

36 ...	Q-Q7
37 K-R2	Q-K6
38 RxP	R-QR1
39 QxQ	

39 P-B5 retained some winning chances.

39 ...	PxQ
40 R-N2	R-R6
41 B-K4	R-B6

The sealed move. The game was **agreed drawn** without resumption. At first Korchnoi feigned horror at Karpov's temerity in offering a draw a pawn down but he was soon persuaded to accept the inevitable.

(Times: 2.37 — 2.26)

GAME TEN

8th August

While the game of musical chairs was still in progress during the ninth game, the Russians distributed their formal reply to my letter on Zukhar in which they denied the hypnosis charges. The day after the ninth game they went on to the offensive and issued a formal protest against Schmid's action regarding Zukhar during the ninth game. The protest was signed by Karpov himself and contained the significant words "It is with regret that I must note that these as well as some other actions on the part of the Chief Arbiter generate doubts as to his objectiveness and impartiality." So the jury met again and after a six (sic!) hour meeting decided that, although he had acted in good faith, Schmid had misinterpreted his powers and that he was not authorised to adjudicate on subjective or mental disturbances — merely on objective or physical ones. This legal nicety would no doubt have delighted A.P. Herbert but it must have seemed to Schmid like a straight reversal of the earlier decision. The official minute of the meeting carefully omits to say what should be done about Zukhar in future! Rumour has it that a gentleman's agreement was reached that Zukhar should not be required to join the rest of the Soviet delegation, but should move back from the fifth to the seventh row. But nobody seems quite sure about this and, not being a gentleman myself, I must confess myself unable to throw light on the matter!

After the meeting Ms. Leeuwerik continued to win over more friends by issuing a statement on behalf of Korchnoi accusing the jury, organisers and president of being pro-Soviet. An extract from this interesting example of international diplomacy will give an indication of its general tone: "Viktor Korchnoi has requested me to say that from now on, until the end of the match, he will be animated by a special feeling when playing the games — he will hear, resounding in the pockets of his adversary, the clank of the chains that fetter his family in the prison camp that is the Soviet Union."

She finished off a busy day by submitting a protest withdrawing her consent to sit in pre-arranged places in the auditorium, demanding that the Russians be searched on entry and insisting that all further draws be offered through the arbiter.

Fortunately the tenth game was sufficiently interesting to divert some attention from the disputes front. It was a close shave for Korchnoi thanks to a startling innovation which apparently emanated from Tal. Korchnoi described Karpov's eleventh move as the kind you find once in a century, and even Golombek was bold enough to declare "It is not a move you see readily. It can easily be overlooked." But Karpov then committed the classic error of attempting to blitz his opponent. Korchnoi gradually outplayed Karpov from a worse ending and gained the upper hand himself. However, Karpov snatched a draw at the end of the session as Korchnoi's time was running out. It was basically an unimpressive game by Karpov who wrongly sacrificed accuracy and artistry for purely practical considerations such as playing quickly.

Karpov now led 1-0 with 9 draws.

White: Karpov
Black: Korchnoi

Ruy Lopez

1 P-K4	P-K4
2 N-KB3	N-QB3
3 B-N5	P-QR3
4 B-R4	N-B3
5 0-0	NxP
6 P-Q4	P-QN4
7 B-N3	P-Q4
8 PxP	B-K3
9 QN-Q2	N-B4
10 P-B3	P-Q5

Consigning 10...P-N3, played in the eighth game, to the scrap heap where it so deservedly belongs. Korchnoi's excuse for that insane move was that he feared Karpov had a theoretical bombshell prepared and in this game it exploded.

11 N-N5 !

As soon as this was played the Soviet delegation exchanged knowing winks and made a move for the bar. Korchnoi was left on the burning deck to work out whether the move was brilliance or bluff. Understandably, after 43 minutes thought, he decided to decline the Russian gift. It remains a open question whether the sacrifice is objectively correct since, perhaps significantly, Karpov did not repeat this variation later in the match.

Here is a selection from the myriad of variations to which the sacrifice could give rise:

A) 11...QxN 12 Q-B3 B-Q2 13 BxPch K-K2! 14 B-Q5 NxKP 15 R-K1 K-Q1 16 RxN QxR 17 BxR B-Q3 18 N-B1 PxP 19 PxP R-B1 with some advantage to Black. But White can improve by 15 Q-K2 with horrible threats, e.g. 15...B-N5 16 N-B3 or 15...P-Q6 16 Q-K1.

B) 11...QxN 12 Q-B3 K-Q2? 13 B-Q5.

C) 11...NxB 12 NxB PxN 13 PxN is rather uncomfortable for Black as he has trouble completing his development.

D) 11...B-Q4 12 NxBP KxN 13

Q-B3ch K-K3 14 Q-N4ch K-K2
(If 14...K-B2 15 Q-B5ch and
P-K6) 15 N-B3 N-K3 16 B-N5
NxB 17 NxN BxB 18 PxB Q-Q4
19 P-QB4 PxP 20 PxP QxBP 21
QR-B1 Q-Q4 22 R-B5 NxP 23
R-K1 QxR 24 Q-K6ch K-Q1 25
N-B7ch NxN 26 Q-K8 mate. A
beautiful variation.

| 11 . . . | PxP |

Safety first, but Black now has a
difficult defensive task ahead.

| 12 NxB | KBPxN |
| 13 PxP | Q-Q6 |

Korchnoi tries to exchange
queens as he does not fear Karpov
in the ending.

14 N-B3?

This eases Black's problem
slightly. 14 P-QB4 was best.

| 14 . . . | QxQ |
| 15 BxQ | |

Of course Karpov wants to keep
the two bishops, but 15 RxQ NxB
16 PxN is more painful for Black
who cannot connect his rooks.
From now on Karpov is steadily
outplayed.

| 15 . . . | B-K2 |

Black does not castle since he
wants to keep his king near the
weakened KP which is in need of
constant protection.

16 B-K3

Better is 16 P-QR4 P-N5 17
B-K3 PxP 18 R-B1 in order to
break up the position for his
bishops.

| 16 . . . | N-Q6 |

Korchnoi now counter-attacks by
exploiting the weakness of White's
KP.

17 B-N3	K-B2
18 QR-Q1	N(6)xKP
19 NxN	NxN
20 B-KB4	N-B5

21 BxN?

Now White's advantage vanishes.
21 R-Q7 was the last chance.

21 . . .	PxB
22 R-Q4	B-Q3
23 B-K3	

K3 was an unlucky square for
Karpov in this game. The text
hands over the initiative to Black
whereas 23 BxB would have
drawn comfortably.

23 . . .	KR-QN1
24 RxP	R-N7
25 P-QR4	R-R7
26 P-N3	R-QN1
27 R-Q1	R(1)-N7
28 R(1)-Q4	R-N8+
29 K-N2	R(8)-R8
30 R-R4	P-R3
31 B-B5	P-K4
32 B-R7	K-K3
33 R(B4)-KN4?	

White's rooks are placed more
clumsily than Black's in any case,
but this crude attempt to blitz
Korchnoi gets Karpov into hot
water. His rook is driven to the
pathetically stupid square KR5.

| 33 . . . | B-K2! |

Did Karpov overlook this?

| 34 R-R5 | B-B3 |

34...B-N4 35 P-R4 P-N3 is too
dangerous. So too is 34...N-N4 35
P-R4 K-B4 36 PxB KxR 37 PxP!
PxP 38 RxKP with too much
compensation for the exchange.

35 R-QB4

| DIAGRAM | |
| 35 . . . | K-Q2? |

35...RxP 36 RxP R-QB8 gives
Black winning chances. In
desperate time trouble Korchnoi
heads for a draw.

36 B-N8	P-B3
37 R-K4	RxRP
38 P-QB4	R-R4

GAME TEN

39	BxP	BxB
40	R(R5)xB	RxR
41	RxR	R-R5
42	R-K4	R-R4
43	P-R4	P-R4
44	R-B4	

Draw agreed

(Times: 1.39 — 2.51)

GAME ELEVEN

The number of protests was now increasing exponentially and rival press conferences were littering all the public buildings.

The Russians issued a reply to Ms. Leeuwerik's inflammatory statement of 8th August. It was entitled "Chess Match in The Philippines Is Not A Training Ground For The Cold War" and contained attacks on Korchnoi, myself and especially Ms. Leeuwerik:

"This woman, who never had anything to do with chess and the international chess movement, who openly declares of her spiteful hatred to the USSR, is trying to convert the distinguished sporting competition, that the World Chess Championship Match is, into the training ground of the Cold War and impede the consolidation of friendship and cultural co-operation, to which admittedly serve chess, between countries."

Even the Chairman of the Jury, Professor Lim Kok Ann joined in the fun, defending himself against Ms. Leeuwerik's accusations of bias and concluding with the words "The Lady doth protest too much, methinks."

Murray Chandler and I diverted ourselves by composing a do-it-yourself protest kit which we were proposing to patent under the brand name 'Gens Una Sumus' the motto of FIDE. In our advertising literature we claimed: "Tests with dummy heads of delegations have proved scientifically that up to 600 protests every 24 hours can be served indiscriminately on match organisers, jury chairmen and chief arbiters."

There was one note of genuine reconciliation. Karpov's accusation of bias against Schmid had not been retracted despite the jury's exoneration of the Chief Arbiter. Schmid was offended and during the tenth game he had a diplomatic illness and his deputy Filip took over. But before the eleventh game he had discussions with Karpov and they issued a joint statement reporting that Karpov now recognised Schmid's impartiality.

In the eleventh game Korchnoi's psychological decision to employ a non-classical opening led to brilliant success. Karpov moved very quickly throughout the whole game, as Golombek put it "... so that he would have plenty of time to regret his errors." The World Champion's middle-game play was extraordinarily pusillanimous and he seemed unable to form a plan. On move 26 he blundered and the rest of the game was a formality. In a way it was a pity that Korchnoi's win should come from this rather easy game instead of one of his more heavyweight creative achievements in earlier games with White.

After the game Korchnoi's group plus Colonel Ed Edmondson and Murray Chandler celebrated at the Pines Hotel with caviar and champagne. Houdini had at last been trapped.

The score was now 1-1 with 9 draws.

White: Korchnoi
Black: Karpov

Sicilian Defence

1 P-KN3	P-QB4
2 B-N2	N-QB3
3 P-K4	P-KN3
4 P-Q3	B-N2
5 P-B4	

We have now reached by transposition a Closed Sicilian Defence, a very unusual opening for a world championship match reminiscent of some Spassky games from 1965 and 1966 in matches against Geller, Larsen and Petrosian.

5 . . .	P-Q3
6 N-KB3	N-B3
7 0-0	0-0
8 P-B3	R-N1
9 Q-K2	

A new plan simply intending to grasp the centre with his pawns. 9 P-KR3 or 9 K-R1 would have been more conventional.

9 . . .	N-K1

Korchnoi favoured 9...P-QN4 10 P-K5 N-Q4 and he even thought Black might then be slightly better.

10 B-K3	N-B2
11 P-Q4	PxP
12 PxP	B-N5
13 R-Q1	P-Q4

Black now becomes cramped and his KB is imprisoned, but if 13... N-K3 14 Q-KB2 Q-N3 15 P-Q5 QxP 16 QN-Q2 wins.

14 P-K5	Q-Q2

15 N-B3	KR-QB1

Better was 15...B-R6 16 B-R1 when Korchnoi planned KR-QB1 followed by N-Q1-B2 to embarrass the far-flung prelate. But after the text Korchnoi seizes the bishop pair, and makes better use of it than Karpov in the previous game.

16 Q-B1	

A fine move to break the pin.

16 . . .	P-QN4
17 P-KR3	BxN

18 BxB

A matter of taste. It was possible to attack on the kingside with 18 QxB P-K3 19 P-KN4 plus N-K2-N3 etc., but Korchnoi observes a subtle possibility to counter-attack on the queenside, which appears to be Black's domain.

Although his pieces appear to be eccentrically placed, they soon start to exhibit a kind of mystical co-operation.

18 . . .	P-N5?

Black should have played 18... P-K3 with equal chances. Karpov

probably overlooked the zwischenzug 19 B-N4 which avoids the
variation 18...P-N5 19 N-R4
NxQP 20 N-B5 NxB with check.
Thus White gains the square QB5
for a knight.

| 19 B-N4 | P-K3 |
| 20 N-R4 | N-R4? |

He had to play 20...B-B1
preparing to surrender the bishop
for White's knight on QB5 which
could have produced a situation
similar to the fifteenth game of
the 1974 match.

| 21 N-B5 | Q-K1 |
| 22 B-K2 | N-N2? |

Feeble. The best chance was the
pawn sacrifice ...N-B5 to obtain
light square control.

23 NxN	RxN
24 R(Q1)-B1	Q-Q2
25 R-B2	P-N6
26 PxP	RxP??

Losing by force. After 26...
R(1)-N1 27 P-QN4 White has an
extra pawn but Black is not
devoid of counterplay.

27 Q-B1!

This neat move not only defends
the bishop on K3 but also
threatens 28 B-R6 to which Black
has no satisfactory answer.
Karpov is therefore forced to
surrender the exchange without
compensation and in a normal
match he would probably have
resigned in a few moves instead of
prolonging the agony.

27 ...	R-N2
28 B-R6	R(1)-N1
29 BxR	RxB
30 R-R3	P-KR3
31 R(R3)-B3	N-N4
32 R-B8+	K-R2
33 R(B2)-B6	P-B3
34 K-N2	Q-KB2
35 Q-B2	P-QR4
36 P-KN4	PxP
37 BPxP	P-R5
38 R-QR8	N-R2
39 R-R6	Q-K2
40 RxRP	R-B2
41 Q-N3	N-B3
42 R-R1	N-N5
43 R-QB1	R-B5
44 R-QN8	

44 RxR PxR 45 QxP Q-N2+ was
best avoided.

44 ...	RxR
45 BxR	Q-QB2
46 RxN	QxB
47 Q-Q3	P-R4
48 R-N6	B-R3
49 PxP	Q-N4+
50 Q-N3	Q-Q7+
51 Q-B2	Black resigns

(Times: 3.16 — 1.41)

GAME TWELVE

15th August

After his loss in game eleven Karpov postponed the twelfth game. In this match each player was entitled to three automatic 'time outs' before game 24. The players had agreed to drop the hypocritical custom which had applied in previous world championship matches, whereby a doctor's certificate was required for a time out but was in fact always granted. What a fruitful source of disputes this could have produced. One can envisage each player demanding that his own doctor examine his opponent and prescriptions of bloodletting etc. being rife.

Philippinos have the endearing habit of calling storms by girls' names and during the lull in hostilities we were visited by tropical storm 'Heling' which forced everyone to stay indoors. AIPE (the International Chess Journalists Association) organised a blitz tournament to keep everyone happy. This was won by Karpov's press secretary Roshal (playing with rather more vigour than the World Champion himself had so far displayed!) ahead of such worthies as Edmondson, Baturinsky, Radoicic and Lothar Schmid's son.

Karpov's rest did not infuse him with much new life and he failed to exploit some over-ambitious play by Korchnoi. Shortly before the adjournment Karpov offered a draw directly to Korchnoi but was merely answered by mute gesticulations. During the adjournment Korchnoi complained to Schmid that Karpov's offer had disturbed him and was contrary to Korchnoi's new policy, announced by Ms. Leeuwerik after the handshake row, that draws must be offered through the arbiter. Schmid misunderstood and thought Korchnoi was offering a draw. He communicated this bogus offer to the Russians and it was accepted. Not wishing to embarrass Schmid, and as the position was drawn anyway, Korchnoi acquiesced in this premature result. It must be the first time that a draw has been offered not through but by the arbiter!

The score was now 1-1 with 10 draws.

White: Karpov
Black: Korchnoi

Ruy Lopez

1 P-K4	P-K4	2 N-KB3	N-QB3
		3 B-N5	P-QR3
		4 B-R4	N-B3
		5 0-0	NxP
		6 P-Q4	P-QN4

7 B-N3	P-Q4
8 PxP	B-K3
9 Q-K2	

Varying from 9 QN-Q2 and 9 P-B3 played in earlier games. The fact that Karpov does not try to repeat the opening of game ten makes one wonder whether the spectacular 11 N-N5 was bluff after all.

9 ...	B-K2
10 R-Q1	0-0
11 P-B4	NPxP
12 BxP	B-QB4
13 B-K3	BxB
14 QxB	Q-N1

I believe this manoeuvre is Korchnoi's own invention.

15 B-N3	N-R4
16 N-K1	

16 ...	Q-N3!

Improving on Hubner-Demarre, Dresden 1969, in which White obtained the advantage after 16... NxB 17 PxN Q-N3 18 QxQ PxQ 19 P-QN4! threatening 20 P-B3. The point of Korchnoi's move order is to avoid the knight being stranded on K5. White has not achieved much from the opening.

17 QxQ	PxQ
18 P-B3	NxB
19 RPxN	N-B4
20 P-QN4	N-Q2

Not 20...N-N6 21 R-R3 P-Q5 22 N-Q2 ultimately winning a pawn.

21 N-Q3	P-KN4?

An incredibly risky move. The point is to cut off lines of communication for White's KP, but it seriously loosens Black's kingside and he eventually loses a pawn.

Korchnoi rejected the plausible 21...P-QR4 because of 22 N-B3 PxP 23 RxR RxR 24 NxNP NxP 25 N(4)xP BxN 26 NxB and White wins a pawn by force. Best was 21...KR-B1 after which the position is about level.

22 N-B3	KR-B1
23 N-B2	P-Q5

A volatile measure designed to avoid White obtaining a good knight on Q4 against Black's bad bishop on K3.

24 N-K2	P-Q6

The only chance to disco-ordinate White's cavalry. If 24...NxP 25 NxP followed by N-K4 and White's centralised knights breathe fire.

25 NxP	B-B5

More accurate is 25...B-N6 26 R-Q2 R-B7 or 25...B-N6 26 R-K1 B-B5 27 N(2)-B1 R-K1 planning ...QR-Q1 followed by ...N-N1-B3-Q5 with full compensation. After the text Black has to struggle a bit.

DIAGRAM

26 N-N3	

This looks suspect. Karpov overlooked Black's 28th move.

If 26 N-B3 P-R3 followed by recapture of the pawn, but 26 P-B4 clinging to the extra material poses more problems, although Korchnoi considered the weakness of White's KP gave good drawing chances.

26 . . .	BxN
27 RxB	NxP
28 R-Q5	N-N3

Before this move Golombek, Panno and I were worried about Black's prospects, but we suddenly realised now that everything was OK.

If 28...P-B3 29 N-K4 K-N2 30 NxP wins.

29 RxP **R-B7**

Black's active pieces (rook on the seventh and possibility of ...N-B5 etc.) guarantee Black near equality. Anyway, as I have stressed before, Korchnoi does not fear Karpov in the ending.

30 P-N3	R-N7
31 N-B5	

31 P-R4 transposes, but 31 P-B4 is somewhat more dangerous.

Now Black liquidates to a total draw.

31 . . .	RxQNP
32 P-R4	K-B1
33 P-R5	N-K2
34 NxN	KxN
35 R-K1+	K-B1
36 R-K4	P-R4
37 R(4)-N4	K-K2
38 PxP	RxRP
39 P-R6	RxR
40 RxR	P-N4
41 R-N7	R-N8+
42 K-R2	R-Q8
43 RxRP	R-Q1
44 R-N7	

44 . . .	R-KR1

The sealed move. The game was **agreed drawn** without resumption. (Times: 2-31 — 2-34)

GAME THIRTEEN

17th and 20th August

Back to the infamous Dr. Zukhar. He was by now again sitting in the fifth row despite the alleged gentleman's agreement that he should sit in the seventh. Whether or not this man really does possess hypnotical or psychological powers or is merely an eccentric-looking quack who enjoys staring at Korchnoi for five hours on end is basically irrelevant. The point is that the Soviets were clearly trying to present a facade of disturbance which the organisers were powerless to prevent since the idiot jury refused to recognise the existence of mental disturbance. Although earlier it had appeared that Petra Leeuwerik was more worried by the staring zombie than Korchnoi, it was now clear that Korchnoi himself had become petrified. His fears were not assuaged by the receipt of an unsolicited academic opinion from Cambridge that hypnosis from a distance is at least possible.

Korchnoi recruited an anti-missile-missile in the person of Israeli psychologist Dr. Vladimir Bergina. Whether he had less powers than Zukhar or whether Karpov is less vulnerable to mental disturbance, Karpov was not in the least put off by Bergina. For some reason Ms. Leeuwerik objected to Bergina's presence. Although he appeared to me be having a beneficial effect on Korchnoi, Ms. Leeuwerik persuaded Korchnoi to send him home after only a few days.

We had by now also obtained the services of Oscar Panno, thinly disguised as a reporter for *Clarion*, the biggest paper in Buenos Aires. And so our secret delegation was beginning to match the Soviet one.

The thirteenth game resumed the unhappy pattern of Korchnoi's encounters with White which had at last been broken in the eleventh game. Korchnoi built up a dominating position, let it slide into equality and then actually lost by a tragic blunder.

He adjourned in what appeared to be a very favourable position. But he wasted a full forty minutes sealing a rather obvious move which only left him 20 minutes for his next 15 moves. I sat glued to my seat for this period going crazy with worry while minutes ticked away. Korchnoi was clearly incredibly nervous and when he had finally decided on the sealed move he put it in the envelope and took it out again several times to make absolutely sure he had written down the move he wanted to play. It was quite obvious to me that he was undergoing acute mental disturbance while trying to seal the move.

After a night of analysis we decided, in view of Korchnoi's time shortage, that it was necessary to take time out for the adjournment session in order to avoid any surprises which might throw him off balance after the adjournment. In retrospect this was the wrong decision. In the extended period of analysis we discovered the position was not a win. It contained good chances but against accurate defence there was very little to be done. This demoralised Korchnoi somewhat. Moreover, before resumption of the thirteenth game, Korchnoi adjourned the fourteenth in a hopeless position and this led him to try desperate and unjustified winning attempts in game thirteen, leading ultimately to his blunder on move 56 in what was by then a totally drawn position.

The thirteenth game reinforced our fear that the Soviet analysts were slightly superior to us. Our analysis was very thorough but theirs had a spark of genius which I suspect was infused by the presence of the brilliant ex-world champion Tal.

Karpov now led 2-1 with 10 draws.

White: Korchnoi
Black: Karpov

Queen's Gambit Declined

1 P-QB4	N-KB3
2 N-QB3	P-K3
3 N-B3	P-Q4
4 P-Q4	B-K2
5 B-N5	P-KR3
6 B-R4	0-0
7 R-B1	P-QN3
8 BxN	BxB
9 PxP	PxP
10 P-KN3	

A new departure. I had analysed this idea in 1968 and Panno played it against Esposito in 1963 in an Argentine club match. But it was Stean who revived the idea and persuaded Korchnoi to use it. At least it avoids the super-solid main lines.

10 . . .	P-B3
11 B-N2	B-B4
12 0-0	Q-Q3
13 P-K3	N-Q2

14 N-K1	KR-K1
15 N-Q3	

Korchnoi based his strategy in this game on the eighth game of his 1977 match with Petrosian. The plan is to exchange off Black's QB and then slowly advance on the queenside to enhance the power of White's fianchettoed KB.

15 . . .   P-N3

I don't like this move much as it cuts off the retreat of the QB. I believe 15...P-QR4 to restrict

73

White's queenside expansion must be better.

16 N-B4	**B-N2**
17 P-KN4	

A bold move, the point of which I did not immediately grasp. Now Black's QB, which defends the light square pawn chain, is exposed to a swap, although White has to pay a small price in the weakening of his king protection.

17 ...	**B-K3**
18 P-KR3	**N-B1**
19 NxB	**NxN**
20 Q-Q3	**QR-Q1**
21 R-B2	**N-B2**

Korchnoi criticised this retreat and recommended ...Q-K2 plus ...Q-R5 and ...N-N4 with more tangible counterplay. I have noticed, however, that Karpov, with Black, tends to play possum in the earlier stages, waiting for the fifth hour and Korchnoi's time trouble before he really comes out and starts a fight.

22 N-R4	**Q-Q2**
23 P-N3	

An interesting speculative piece sacrifice is 23 P-N4 P-QB4 24 NPxP QxN 25 PxP N-K3 26 P-N7. It could also be tried next move when Black's knight can no longer go to K3.

23 ...	**R-K3**
24 N-B3	**R-Q3**
25 P-N4	**B-B1**
26 N-K2	**P-QN4**

Trying to get his knight to QB5. But Korchnoi has enough time to undermine Black's queenside structure first.

27 Q-N3	**N-R1**
28 P-QR4	**PxP**

If 28...P-R3 29 P-R5 and the

knight is incarcerated.

29 QxRP	**N-N3**
30 Q-N3	**R-N1**
31 N-B4	**N-B5**
32 Q-R4	**P-KB4**

Typical Karpov — a move in the same league as his 33...P-R4 in game nine. He chooses just the right moment psychologically and practically to randomise the position. Objectively I feel Black is now hovering near the brink of defeat, but it takes a great effort to push him over, and meanwhile Korchnoi was getting tired and the clock was ticking away precious minutes.

33 PxP	**QxP**
34 QxRP	**RxP**
35 R-R2	**Q-B1**
36 R-B1	**R-N2**
37 Q-R4?	

This I do not understand. Why not 37 Q-R6 putting the queen in a more active position and pinning Black's rook? If queens are exchanged White will drive off Black's well placed knight with B-B1, with potentially overwhelming pressure against Black's queenside pawns.

37 ...	**R-KB2**

Black has successfully consolidated his scattered forces and

White's advantage is now in question. In fact his best chance is the following exchange sacrifice.

38 RxN	PxR
39 QxP(4)	Q-B4
40 N-Q3	B-N2

41 R-R7

The sealed move over which Korchnoi thought for so long.

| 41 ... | R(3)-B3 |

Probably best, although Black has a huge number of playable alternatives which are very hard to crack, such as 41...P-R4 or even the retraction 41...B-B1, now that White's KB2 is no longer protected. This complicated our task of analysis. It also transpired that White could never win if the queens and one rook each were exchanged.

42 RxR

42 N-K5 allows 43...QxP+ drawing.

| 42 ... | RxR |

43 P-Q5

It seemed more aggressive to push the pawn to QB6 but this allows a black square blockade and so simply 43 BxP was better.

| 43 ... | B-K4 |

A fine resource which prevents White's king reaching safety at KR2. Now Korchnoi should have given up trying to win.

44 PxP	K-N2
45 B-K4	Q-N4+
46 K-B1	B-Q3
47 B-Q5	R-K2
48 B-B3	P-R4
49 B-Q1	Q-KB4
50 K-K2	R-K5
51 Q-B3+	Q-B3
52 Q-N3	Q-B4
53 Q-N7+	

Rashly rejecting repetition by 53 Q-B3+.

53 ...	R-K2
54 Q-N2+	K-R2
55 Q-Q4	B-B2

56 Q-KR4??

With only one move to go to the time control, White throws the game away.

| 56 ... | R-K5 |
| 57 P-B4 | |

The only way to save the trapped queen, but now White's position collapses.

57 ...	B-N3
58 B-B2	RxP+
59 K-Q2	Q-R4+
60 K-Q1	Q-R8+
61 K-Q2	R-K5

White resigned.

(Times: 3-58 — 3-56)

GAME FOURTEEN

19th and 20th August

The fourteenth game, started in the interval between the first and second sessions of the thirteenth, witnessed yet another Open Variation of the Ruy Lopez. Earlier in the match this had served Korchnoi well and he had the advantage that he had access to Kevin O'Connell's new book on this opening while Karpov was relying on Korchnoi's contribution to *The Encyclopedia of Chess Openings* published in 1974 and now becoming out of date. Korchnoi had likened Karpov's conduct of the opening to a pupil learning his lesson and then being confronted by his teacher for the examination. But latterly the pupil had been going outside the syllabus and embarrassed his teacher with awkward questions in games 8, 10 and 12.

Once again Karpov got the better position from the opening but Korchnoi had a defensible position when he overlooked a simple exchange sacrifice. Initially Karpov only obtained one pawn for his investment but, following another mistake by Korchnoi, further dividends were declared. In the second session, played immediately after Korchnoi's debacle in the thirteenth game Karpov rapidly registered his second win of the day. The game illustrated Karpov's skill at exploiting small advantages in an unspectacular but effective manner.

Karpov now led 3-1 with 10 draws.

White: Karpov
Black: Korchnoi

Ruy Lopez

1 P-K4	P-K4
2 N-KB3	N-QB3
3 B-N5	P-QR3
4 B-R4	N-B3
5 0-0	NxP
6 P-Q4	P-QN4
7 B-N3	P-Q4
8 PxP	B-K3
9 P-B3	B-QB4
10 QN-Q2	0-0
11 B-B2	B-B4
12 N-N3	B-KN5
13 P-KR3	

A new departure which is actually the most straightforward attempt to refute Black's opening. Black could have tried a pseudo-Dilworth sacrifice with 13...BxN 14 PxB NxKBP 15 RxN BxR+ 16 KxB NxP but after my suggestion 17 Q-N1! White is still on top, e.g. 17...R-K1 18 B-N5 Q-Q3 19 Q-N3 N-N5+ 20 BPxN R-K7+ 21 K-B3 QxQ+ 22 KxQ

RxB 23 N-Q4 RxNP 24 B-B1 winning.

13 ...	B-R4
14 P-N4	B-KN3

Korchnoi assesses this position as unclear in ECO but it soon becomes evident that White will exert a permanent dark square grip.

15 BxN	PxB
16 NxB	PxN
17 B-B4	QxQ

If 17...Q-K2 18 Q-Q5 N-R4 19 P-N4 Black's front KBP is ultimately doomed and this, combined with White's control of space, would give White a distinct advantage.

18 QRxQ	N-Q1
19 R-Q7	N-K3
20 NxN	PxN
21 B-K3	QR-B1
22 KR-Q1	

Also excellent is 22 B-B5 KR-K1 23 R-K1 playing to exclude Black's bishop from the game. Karpov had been moving very rapidly and I feared, justifiably, that he had prepared the variation far into the ending. Since Black does not have a wide choice in his cramped quarters, this would not have been too difficult a task for him.

22 ...	B-K5
23 B-B5	KR-K1
24 R(7)-Q4	B-Q4
25 P-N3	P-QR4
26 K-R2	R-R1
27 K-N3	R-R3?

Commencing a faulty manoeuvre which overlooks entirely that Black can sacrifice the exchange. The best chance was 27...B-B3 followed by ...P-R5 though it would still not be easy for Black.

28 P-KR4	R-B3

29 RxB!

Of course. For some inexplicable reason Korchnoi had not even considered this.

29 ...	PxR
30 RxP	R(3)-K3
31 B-Q4	P-B3
32 R-B5	R-KB1?

Usually I watched the games from the press centre, but today I was invited to give a speech at the closing ceremony of the Philippino championship, which was also held in Baguio. During the speech I was handed a note with this position from the game on it. I saw at once that Black had to play 32...R-Q1 33 KxP R-Q4 and if 34 K-K4 R(K3)xKP+. White's only chance to play for a win would be 34 RxR PxR, although with one rook exchanged and Black's K5 in his control Black should hold the position.

After the text Black goes irrevocably downhill.

33 P-R4	PxP
34 PxP	P-N3
35 RxRP	R(3)-K1
36 R-R7	R-B2
37 R-R6	R-B2
38 B-B5	R(2)-B1
39 B-Q6	R-R1
40 RxP	RxRP
41 KxP	P-R4

DIAGRAM

The adjourned position which is easily won for White.

42 PxP	PxP
43 P-B4	R-R7
44 R-N6	K-B2
45 P-B5	R-R5
46 P-B6	K-K3
47 P-B7	K-Q2

48 R-N8	R-QB1
49 K-K3	

Not at once 49 P-K6+ KxP 50 RxP KxB.

49 . . .   RxRP

In view of the threat of P-B4, P-B5 etc. Black has nothing better.

50 P-K6+   Black resigns

50...KxP now fails to the *zwischenzug* 51 B-N3.

(Times: 2-48 − 2-54)

GAME FIFTEEN

When the thirteenth game was adjourned Korchnoi had appeared to have good chances of going 2-1 up but now he was suddenly 3-1 down. The gods could not let such a dramatic reversal go unnoticed so they chose to mark the occasion by means of an earthquake of force six on the Richter Scale (I am not sure what the equivalent Elo rating is). Lightning even penetrated Harry Golombek's bedroom. Why the gods chose to pick on this innocent bystander I don't know, but fortunately he was unharmed.

Although shaken by his recent experiences Korchnoi decided not to postpone the fifteenth game. However, the game was a limp affair and the first time since the first game that Korchnoi failed to make any impression with White. He played the Catalan for the first time in the match and was confronted by a sharp pawn sacrifice which Karpov had obviously prepared beforehand. Naturally wishing to steady his nerves after Sunday's disaster, Korchnoi did not try to refute the sacrifice by hanging on to the pawn and the game rapidly petered out into a draw.

The only excitement was provided by an altercation on stage when Karpov started rocking his chair, which drew forth sharp words from Korchnoi. A jury meeting the following morning decided that such disturbances would henceforth be forbidden.

Karpov now led 3-1 with 11 draws.

White: Korchnoi
Black: Karpov

Catalan Opening

1 P-QB4	N-KB3
2 N-QB3	P-K3
3 N-B3	P-Q4
4 P-Q4	B-K2
5 P-KN3	0-0
6 B-N2	PxP
7 N-K5	N-B3

An odd looking move which saddles Black with tripled pawns.

The point is that White has to waste time capturing these and Black is happy to sacrifice a pawn for a lead in development.

8 BxN	PxB
9 NxP(B6)	Q-K1
10 NxB+	QxN
11 Q-R4	P-B4
12 QxBP	PxP
13 QxQP	P-K4
14 Q-KR4	R-N1
15 B-N5	

An unambitious move. White

79

could have put Black's opening sacrifice to the test by trying to hold on to the pawn with 15 P-QR3 or 15 0-0 R-N5 16 Q-N5 etc.

    15 . . .   **RxP**

16 . . .	**Q-K3**
17 BxN	**QxB**
18 QxQ	**PxQ**
19 QR-N1	**RxR**
20 RxR	**B-K3**
21 P-B3	**R-B1**
22 R-QB1	**R-N1**
23 R-B2	**R-QB1**
24 K-B2	**BxP**
25 RxB	

16 0-0
White could have settled for a draw at once with 16 N-Q5 Q-N2 17 NxN+ PxN 18 0-0 PxB 19 QxNP+. He might as well have done so as the text also leads to a clearly drawn position.

Draw agreed
(Times: 1-28 — 0-52)

GAME SIXTEEN

24th August

The weather continued to cast a damper on the proceedings. It rained twenty-four hours a day and even the fish were drowning. Two people were actually killed by a landslide at the back of the playing hall. Rain streamed through the hotel roof and Stean aquired a private lake in his bedroom. Not being able to swim he chose to evacuate.

There were fears that the generator in the playing hall might collapse and the sixteenth game have to be postponed but Campomanes gave the green light. After the game the generator at the Pines Hotel did indeed explode and we were plunged into darkness for hours. I was interested to learn that the Philippinos picturesquely describe such events as brown-outs.

After much pleading from his seconds Korchnoi finally dropped the Open Ruy Lopez for the sixteenth game. To be honest his choice of the French was as much a surprise to his seconds as it must have been to Karpov. We were planning a different half-open defence but at the last minute Korchnoi discovered a flaw in our analysis and so resorted to the French Defence without much prior analysis, relying on his great experience with this opening to pull him through.

Korchnoi's choice of opening was a success. Karpov was obviously not expecting the line Korchnoi played and missed the best continuation on move 12. He retained a slight advantage but Korchnoi defended adequately and the game was adjourned in a drawn position which was not resumed.

The Tarrasch Variation which Karpov plays against the French gives Black very few chances of winning and it may be for this reason that Korchnoi had not allowed it before. However, it simplifies the position to such an extent that Black should be able to draw by suitably patient defence and so it is not ideal for a match such as this where a draw can always be regarded as a satisfactory result for Black. Perhaps, therefore, Korchnoi should have adopted the French Defence earlier, but the spectators can be grateful he did not in view of the seven tedious draws the opening led to in the 1974 match.

Karpov now led 3-1 with 12 draws.

White: Karpov
Black: Korchnoi

French Defence

1 P-K4	P-K3
2 P-Q4	P-Q4
3 N-Q2	P-QB4
4 KPxP	KPxP
5 B-N5+	

In the 1974 match Karpov had invariably played 5 KN-B3 and the games continued 5...N-QB3 6 B-N5.

| 5 . . . | B-Q2 |

Karpov seemed surprised by this move. Was he expecting 5...N-B3 6 KN-B3 transposing back into the lines played in the 1974 match? If so, why did he play 5 B-N5ch rather than 5 KN-B3?

| 6 Q-K2+ | Q-K2 |

In the twenty-second game Korchnoi played the more complicated alternative 6 . . . B-K2 but also failed to equalise.

7 BxB+	NxB
8 PxP	NxP
9 N-N3	QxQ+
10 NxQ	NxN
11 RPxN	B-B4

12 B-Q2

Better is 12 N-B3 which leads to a plus for White after either 12 . . .

N-B3 13 N-R4 or 12 . . . 0-0-0 13 R-R5 (Hort-Ivkov, Wijk aan Zee 1970).

12 . . .	N-K2
13 N-B4	0-0
14 0-0	KR-Q1
15 N-Q3	B-N3
16 P-B3	P-B3
17 KR-Q1	K-B2
18 K-B1	N-B4?

Black immediately has to retract this careless move which withdraws support from the vulnerable QP. 18...N-B3 would have been quite satisfactory, especially as it prevents 19 N-N4.

19 B-K1	N-K2
20 N-N4	R-Q2
21 R-Q3	QR-Q1
22 QR-Q1	K-K3
23 B-Q2	N-B3

At this stage I thought Black had comfortable equality, but my optimism was dispelled by Karpov's next few moves. By impressively accurate play he maintained his grip and lured Black's rook to the horribly passive square QN3.

24 NxN	PxN
25 P-QN4	K-B2
26 B-K3	BxB
27 RxB	R-QN1
28 R-K2	R-N4
29 R-R1	R(Q2)-N2
30 R-Q2	K-K3
31 R-R6	R(N4)-N3
32 R-R2	K-Q3
33 K-K2	R-K2+
34 K-Q3	P-QR3

DIAGRAM

| 35 R-Q1? | |

Karpov succumbs to his besetting sin of trying to blitz Korchnoi and throws away most of his advantage

opportunities for manoeuvring.

36 . . .	K-Q1
37 P-B3	R-K4
38 K-Q4	K-B2
39 R-K1	K-Q3
40 P-KB4	RxR
41 RxR	P-QR4
42 PxP	RxP

The sealed move. The game was agreed drawn during the adjournment.

by a hasty move. Better alternatives would have been 35 P-KN3 or 35 R-K2 swapping Black's active rook and leaving him with the miserable beast on QN3.

35 . . .	K-B2

36 R(R2)-R1

36 R(Q1)-R1 followed by R-R4, P-QN3 and eventually P-B4 would still have left White with some

A plausible continuation at the end would have been 43 R-QR1 P-B4+ 44 K-Q3 R-N2 45 P-R6 R-R2 46 P-B4 P-Q5 47 R-R5 K-B3 48 P-N3 and if 48...K-N3 49 R-N5+ etc. White can also draw by leaving his rook on QR1 meeting ...K-N3 with R-N1+ KxP R-N5 R-B2 creating a totally drawn position a pawn down.

(Times: 2-12 — 2-32)

GAME SEVENTEEN

26th August

The Zukhar dispute had been quietly simmering during the last few games. The main development was Ms. Leeuwerik's new habit of trying to distract him by kicking his shins and jabbing the small of his back with a pen. This approach was less successful than the more subtle *Gulag Archipelago* Gambit she had adopted earlier, and Ms. Leeuwerik's only success was to make an exhibition of herself.

Now the dispute really boiled over again. At the beginning of the game Korchnoi objected violently to Zukhar's presence and threatened to evict him by physical violence if necessary. Eventually Campomanes agreed to move him back but warned that this would be the last time.

The seventeenth game was yet another tragedy for Korchnoi. Following the familiar pattern he built up a won position with White after improving on his play in game seven. His position in the early middle game was so good that he retained winning chances even after a number of inaccuracies in the later middle game. But he no longer had winning chances when disaster struck: Korchnoi allowed an elegant but obvious mate in three. His resignation was greeted by singing and screaming from thirty tourists who had fortuitously arrived from Russia that day. This must have taken Korchnoi's mind back to the partisan crowds who watched his 1974 match against Karpov in Moscow.

Korchnoi had wasted thirteen precious minutes on his clock by his fulminations against Zukhar at the start of the game. Perhaps forgetting this he commented after the game: "I don't know where my time went. I thought I was moving quickly." Would the extra thirteen minutes have been enough time to allow Korchnoi to have won his overwhelming position? Thirteen seconds should have sufficed to at least avoid the loss at the end.

After each win Karpov had a party and this time the Terraces Plaza Hotel presented him with a cake showing the final position of the seventeenth game. The first thing he did was eat White's king!

Karpov now led 4-1 with 12 draws.

White: Korchnoi		
Black: Karpov	1 P-QB4	N-KB3
	2 N-QB3	P-K3
Nimzo-Indian Defence	3 P-Q4	B-N5

4 P-K3	0-0
5 B-Q3	P-B4
6 P-Q5	P-QN4

Repeating the sharp method adopted in the seventh game. This may not in fact be the best move. The paradoxical 6...P-KR3, which bypasses the possibility of BxRP+ and leaves White with some anxiety about his centre, e.g. 7 P-K4 PxP 8 KPxP BxN+ 9 PxB R-K1+ 10 N-K2 P-Q3 and the position is about equal.

7 PxKP	BPxP
8 PxP	P-QR3

Varying from 8...B-N2 played in the seventh game.

9 N-K2

Improving his strategy in the seventh game when he developed this knight on KB3.

9 ...	P-Q4
10 0-0	P-K4
11 P-QR3	PxP
12 BxNP	BxN
13 PxB	B-R3
14 R-N1	Q-Q3
15 P-QB4	P-Q5
16 N-N3	

By now it was clear that Karpov's handling of the opening had been inauspicious to say the least. I felt that Black was already lost. Not only was he a pawn down,

but his own centre pawns were not mobile and there were a number of weak squares in his camp, such as KB4.

16 ...	N-B3
17 P-QR4	N-QR4
18 Q-Q3	Q-K3
19 PxP	BPxP
20 P-B5	KR-B1
21 P-B4	

21 B-N5 is a good alternative, but the text, ripping open lines against Black's insecure kingside, is quite sufficient to win.

21 ...	RxP
22 BxB	QxB
23 QxQ	

Better was 23 R-N8+ K-B2 24 R-N5 displacing Black's king, keeping queens on the board and introducing unpleasant threats such as PxP and Q-B5. Incredibly Korchnoi did not even consider this obvious manoeuvre and from now on we witness his decline.

23 ...	RxQ
24 B-R3	R-Q4
25 N-B5	K-B2
26 PxP	RxP
27 R-N5?	

This is a blunder which allows Black to complicate things in White's time pressure. Again the simple course would have been 27

NxQP and White still has good chances to win.

Down in the press room I was beginning to become pessimistic.

| 27 ... | N-B5 |

A typical example of Karpov's eel-like defensive skill after earlier unimpressive play. If now 28 N-Q6+ RxN 29 RxR R-Q2 and the Black knight on QB5 is forking two pieces.

28 R-N7+	K-K3
29 NxQP+	K-Q4
30 N-B3?	

Better was 30 B-B8 KxN 31 BxP R(K)-K3 32 R-B7 K-K4 33 P-N4 P-R3 34 R-B5+ or 33...N-K6 34 R(B1)xN RxR 35 P-N5 and wins. In view of this Black would have to play 31...N-K5. White can then get rook plus pawns for two knights in much more favourable circumstances than the game. All this was proposed by Murei.

Perhaps the simplest, however, was the line proposed by Panno: 30 N-B2 NxB 31 N-N4+ or 30 N-B2 RxP 31 B-B8 and Black is still in deep water.

30 ...	NxB
31 NxR	KxN
32 R-K7+	K-Q5
33 RxP	N-B5
34 R-B4+	

Better was 34 R-B7.

34 ...	N-K5
35 R-Q7+	K-K6
36 R-B3+	K-K7
37 RxP	N(B)-Q7
38 R-QR3	R-QB3
39 R-R1??	

Now the 'kremlins' get at White's position. 39 P-R4 also lost to 39... R-B8+ 40 K-R2 N-B8+ 41 K-R3 N-B7 mate. But simply 39 P-N4 should draw since after 39... N-B6+ 40 RxN KxR 41 P-R4 the ending is still drawn even if Black wins all White's pawns.

| 39 ... | N-B6+! |

Very pretty. It is mate after 40 K-R1 N-B7 or 40 PxN R-N2+ 41 K-R1 N-B7.

White therefore resigned.

(Times: 2-28 – 2-92)

GAME EIGHTEEN

2nd and 3rd September

Korchnoi was now trailing 1-4 and his position appeared desperate. Nobody since Steinitz in 1886 had yet won a world championship after being three games down, though as recently as 1954 Smyslov managed at least to draw his match against Botvinnik after starting with one draw and three losses. Korchnoi's main consolation was that, as the match was of unlimited duration, Karpov needed to win two more games and so could not canter home with draws as he had done in the 1974 match. Nonetheless Korchnoi's task of winning five games while conceding only one loss was a daunting one.

Many people were predicting that Korchnoi would now find a pretext for defaulting the match rather than suffer the indignity of defending a hopeless cause. I never gave much credence to this fear for two reasons. Firstly Korchnoi disapproves in principle of not fighting out to the bitter end, as witnessed by his expressions of contempt for Spassky's action in threatening to walk out of the Candidates' final. Secondly the loser's prize offered 100,000 good reasons for completing the match! The joker in the pack was Ms. Leeuwerik. She clearly had considerable influence over Korchnoi and I was afraid that, if she thought that Korchnoi could no longer win the match, she might regard a political bust-up as a more satisfactory end to the match than a clear-cut chess victory for Karpov. Despite our disagreement on policy Ms. Leeuwerik and I remained on good terms personally. We both wanted what we thought was best for Korchnoi but we happened to disagree radically on how this should be achieved.

The day after the seventeenth game we were sidetracked by rather a trivial issue. Despite our defeat over the flag issue Ms. Leeuwerik was still insisting that our delegation be referred to as the Swiss delegation rather than the Korchnoi delegation. Lim Kok Ann sent a telegram to the Swiss Chess Federation asking two questions — 1. Did Ms. Leeuwerik represent Korchnoi only or the Swiss Chess Federation itself? 2. If she did represent the Swiss Chess Federation did they accept responsibility for her "violent political statements" and "damaging allegations"? The Swiss Chess Federation merely answered the second question, denying responsibility, and left the first question unanswered. There was a meeting to discuss the matter which I attended in the Gilbertian dual capacity of translator and chief second. Inside the jury room I was translator but I had to leave the chamber occasionally and revert to my role as chief second to sign certain documents. At one time a fog from rain outside penetrated our deliberations which added to the unreal nature of the proceedings. In the end I managed to have the whole silly matter suppressed without a vote.

Korchnoi now decided to take two 'time-outs' before the eighteenth game. This was a gamble. It meant that he would not be entitled to any more postponements unless the match lasted for more than 24 games. But it also gave Korchnoi a chance to recharge his batteries (and Karpov his Batuniskys?) and make a fresh start.

Korchnoi chose to take his rest in Manila rather than Baguio and he flew off there with Ms. Leeuwerik. In her absence I was appointed acting head of the Korchnoi delegation and I was determined to make the most of this opportunity. By now I was convinced that Ms. Leeuwerik had not been acting in Korchnoi's best interests. She seemed more intent on using the match as a political platform for attacking the Russians rather than squashing side-issues which might distract Korchnoi and so enabling him to give of his best in the match.

In my new role as head of the Korchnoi delegation I attended a meeting to reconsider the Zukhar question. I decided to follow R.A. Butler's maxim that politics is the art of the possible and approached the meeting in a concilatory mood. I started the meeting by ordering a round of drinks and Baturinsky mellowed considerably. He very soon agreed that Zukhar should sit at the back of the Playing Hall with the rest of the Soviet delegation, which was all we had ever wanted from our negotia- tions. The only concession we had to make in exchange was that Korchnoi should stop wearing the special proplylactic reflective glasses which he had been wearing even before the Zukhar controversy arose. Why Karpov should find his own reflection disturbing I don't know, but the glasses had been giving Korchnoi headaches anyway and so this point was readily agreed. The joint communiqué issued by Baturinsky and myself concluded: "The participants' representatives have expressed their hope that all this will contribute to the further course of the match in the interest of chess and in the spirit of FIDE principles".

I was happy to have settled in one meeting the problem which had defied solution for five weeks. I was flattered when Panno wrote comparing me to Disraeli, assuming that the more seedy machinations of that student of Machiavelli have not found their way into the Argentinian history books. But I was brought down from the clouds by the news that Korchnoi had just given a press conference in Manila threatening to walk out of the match unless the organisers installed a one-way mirror in the Playing Hall which would allow the audience to see the players, but not the players the audience. I hastily despatched a delegation consisting of Stean Murei and Edmondson to Manila to inform Korchnoi that the war was over and prevent him from continuing hostilities in ignorance of this conclusion, like Japanese cut off in the jungle after World War II. Fortunately their counsels prevailed. Korchnoi withdrew his new demands and my original compromise was reinstated. Although Edmondson was not an official member of our delegation he proved himself a tower of strength, no doubt drawing on his experience in persuading that other turbulent genius, Fischer, to play in 1972, and so I continued in charge of negotiations. Michael Stean commented on this takeover: 'It was a bloodless coup. Petra's exuberance has lost us much goodwill'.

Twenty minutes before the start of the eighteenth game I summoned an informal meeting of the jury and, toasting peace, expressed the hope that our future meetings would be over drinks and not over protests. I also presented olive branches in the form of carved wooden horses to all.

The audience for the eighteenth game was swelled by the august presence of the USSR ambassador. He originally sat in the second row but after a brief discussion with Camponanes I had him moved to join the rest of the Soviet delegation before the start of play. After all the problems in shifting Zukhar I was very pleased to be able to shift the USSR ambassador in two minutes.

In the eighteenth game Korchnoi played the Pirc Defence for the first time in the match. This was in accordance with our policy of chopping and changing his defences with Black in order to sidetrack Karpov's preparation. Unfortunately Karpov got in with a novelty first. Korchnoi slipped into a slightly dubious middle game and only succeeded in saving himself after adjournment by some fine endgame play. None-the-less, this was a reasonable achievement considering he had spent the preceding week in Manila issuing ultimatums rather than preparing for the game. Afterwards Tal praised Korchnoi's defensive skill in a difficult situation.

Karpov now led 4-1, with 13 draws.

White: Karpov
Black: Korchnoi

Pirc Defence

1 P-K4	P-Q3
2 P-Q4	N-KB3
3 N-QB3	P-KN3
4 N-B3	

Recently Karpov has invariably played the Two Knights variation against the Pirc Defence rather than one of the more aggressive systems beginning with 4 P-B4

Korchnoi's own high point with this opening was his win against Fischer in the Candidates' tournament in 1962.

4 . . .	B-N2
5 B-K2	0-0
6 0-0	B-N5
7 B-K3	N-B3
8 Q-Q3	

Karpov has made a specialty of 8 Q-Q2 in this position — see for example his games against

Timman at Tilburg 1977 and against Adorjan at Las Palmas 1977. The idea of this new move is to have the square Q2 available for the king's knight. Korchnoi pondered for fifteen minutes over his reply.

| 8 ... | P-K4 |
| 9 P-Q5 | N-N5 |

Korchnoi spent a further twenty minutes on this move. The alternative is 9 ... N-K2 10 N-Q2 B-Q2 11 N-B4 N-K1 12 P-B4 when white has the advantage as black cannot manoeuvre a knight towards K4.

| 10 Q-Q2 | P-QR4 |
| 11 P-KR3 | |

Korchnoi was more afraid of 11 N-K1. The exchange of the light square bishops whould then help White in view of the fixed central pawn chain. But if Black's QB retreats then 12 P-QR3 followed by 13 N-Q3 shuts Black's QN out of the game for a long time.

Karpov used sixteen minutes here so he was obviously out of his prepared line.

| 11 ... | B-Q2 |
| 12 B-KN5 | |

More unpleasant for Black is 12 P-R3 N-R3 13 QR-N1 intending P-QN4 when Black's knight on QR3 is a liability. If then 13. . . N-B4 14 BxN PxB 15 NxP is good for White.

| 12 ... | Q-K1 |
| 13 N-R2 | |

13 N-K1 was a better method of preparing for . . . P-KB4 than this decentralisation.

13 ...	K-R1
14 P-R3	N-R3
15 B-R6	BxB

| 16 QxB | N-KN1? |

This prepares an incorrect plan. Korchnoi overestimates the virtues of . . . P-KB4 which turns out merely to create weaknesses. Black could have equalised by 16 . . . N-B4 17 Q-K3 P-B3 e.g. 18 P-QN4 PxQP 19 PxN P-Q5 20 Q-Q3 PxN 21 PxP B-B3 and Black will easily surround the White pawn on Q3.

17 Q-K3	P-KB4
18 PxP	BxP
19 QR-B1	N-B3
20 P-KN4!	

An excellent move over which Karpov spent twenty-five minutes. The fact that he can continue to dominate Black's QN and QB outweighs any slight weaknesses in his own camp. This move is typical of Karpov's skill in positions where he has a space advantage.

20 ...	B-Q2
21 P-B4	PxP
22 QxP	N-B4
23 QR-K1	

We were more worried by 23 Q-Q4 Q-K4 (not 23 . . . QN-K5 24 RxN! RxR 25 P-N5) 24 QxQ PxQ 25 N-B3

| 23 ... | KN-K5 |
| 24 Q-K3 | Q-K4 |

25 NxN	NxN
26 B-B3	N-N4

The only chance is to simplify. 26 . . . Q-N6+? would lead Black to an impasse.

27 QxQ	PxQ

Now Black's weak KP guarantees White a small but lasting advantage.

28 B-N2	RxR+
29 NxR	R-K1
30 N-Q2	P-R5
31 R-K3	

Karpov decides not to rush matters by 31 P-B4 or 31 N-K4 and instead plays for the adjournment — rather a surprising decision as Korchnoi only had thirteen minutes for his next ten moves.

31 . . .	K-N2
32 K-B2	R-K2
33 P-B4	P-N3
34 R-QB3	P-R4

By exchanging a pair of pawns on the kingside, Black prevents White from later expanding there by P-R4 and P-N5.

35 K-N3	PxP
36 PxP	B-K1
37 P-B5	PxP
38 N-K4	NxN
39 BxN	K-B3
40 RxP	K-N4

The adjourned positions. White clearly has a pull as Black's pieces are passive and there are a number of vulnerable pawns in his camp, but I thought at first it would not be too difficult to hold. Korchnoi even opined that this was the best positon he had had for the whole game. However we gradually became more and more pessimistic as the active plans for Black (such as playing for . . . R-KB5) all seemed too dangerous. Korchnoi does not like to defend passively but eventually the decision was taken to do as little as possible. Over the next eight moves White plays non-committally hoping that Black will become active but Korchnoi did not oblige.

41 B-Q3	R-B2
42 B-K2	R-R2
43 B-B3	R-B2
44 R-B4	R-R2
45 R-N4	R-K2
46 K-B2	B-Q2
47 K-N3	B-K1
48 K-B2	B-Q2
49 K-K3	

White gets moving at last but Black is ready.

49 . . .	P-K5

The correct moment to obtain a passed KNP.

50 BxP	KxP
51 K-B2	K-N4
52 B-B2	R-K4
53 BxRP	BxB
54 RxB	RxP
55 K-K3	R-N4
56 P-N4	R-K4+
57 K-Q4	K-B5
58 R-R8	P-N4
59 R-QB8	R-K5+
60 K-Q5	R-K4+
61 K-B6	P-N5

62 RxP	P-N6
63 K-N6	P-N7
64 R-B1	K-B6

DIAGRAM

Draw agreed. A possible conclusion would have been 65 P-R4 K-B7 66 P-R5 R-K8 67 R-B2+ R-K7 68 R-B1 R-K8 69 R-B2+ with a draw by repetition. If Black forces White to give up his rook in this variation by 67 . . . K-B8 the position is still drawn after e.g. 68 RxP KxR 69 P-R6 R-QR8 70 P-R7 K-B6 71 K-N7 K-K5 72 P-R8=Q

RxQ 73 KxR K-Q4 and Black wins White's last pawn.

(Times: 4.02 — 4.07)

GAME NINETEEN

After the eighteenth game the new spirit of détente was marked by a party given for both delegations by the wife of President Marcos. She had recently been nominated for the Nobel Peace prize and on the evidence of this occasion she certainly deserved it. It was a pity that adverse weather conditions prevented her from attending the party herself.

The party started a little frostily but as the evening wore on the two delegations began to intermingle. Everyone obviously enjoyed themselves and by the end of the evening even the sinister Dr. Zukhar was to be observed in a tired and parapsychological condition happily dancing to the strains of Mozart and Liszt.

When dawn broke there were obviously those who wished it hadn't, and the Russians decided to postpone the nineteenth game. This may seem rather surprising as the game was not due to start till 5 p.m., but Karpov had two postponements in reserve before game 24 and so he could easily afford to use one of them.

For the nineteenth game Ms. Leeuwerik flooded the audience with parapsychologists and gurus, thus brilliantly solving the problem of the sparse audience for the match.

One group consisted of girl parapsychology students of Father Jaime Bulatao the Jesuit priest from Ateneo de Manila University. They were an ornamental addition to the audience and Korchnoi had reason to be grateful that he had not pressed his demand for a one-way mirror. This nubile bunch was busy conjuring up good vibrations for Korchnoi, though it later transpired that none of them could play chess. It was charming to watch them thinking positively and willing Korchnoi to victory in positions where a draw was all he could reasonably hope for.

The other group, who appeared to be rivals of the first, was composed of two members of the fanatical religious sect Ananda Marga, called Stephen Dwyer and Victoria Shepherd. Resplendent in saffron robes and turbans they adopted the lotus position in the immediate vicinity of the Soviet delegation. This colourful couple were on bail pending appeal against conviction for the attempted murder, by stabbing, of a diplomat, for which they had each received a seventeen year sentence. It was therefore readily understandable that the Russians swiftly evacuated their benches and trooped *en masse* into the restaurant in the bowels of the Convention Centre. The picturesque pair were later persuaded to move a few seats away from the Soviet enclosure so that the Russians could return. As soon as they complied they were encircled by security agents who kept them under nervous surveillance for the rest of the game.

Before the match Korchnoi had predicted that it would be over in twenty games. When the nineteenth game started, Karpov needed only two more wins to retain his title. Did Korchnoi remember his earlier prediction?

The course of the nineteenth game suggests that Korchnoi was still trying to consolidate his nerves after earlier traumatic experiences. He adopted the Catalan Opening with which he had obtained no advantage in the fifteenth game. Again Karpov equalised comfortably and it seemed to me, from the amount of time Korchnoi took over the early phase of the game, that Korchnoi was not entirely at ease. The game fluctuated slightly but it was always objectively drawn and Korchnoi's only real danger came from his old enemy the clock. But he managed to find some good moves fast and shortly before the adjournment the game was agreed drawn by means of a mutual shrug of the shoulders.

Karpov now led 4-1, with 14 draws.

White: Korchnoi
Black: Karpov

Catalan Opening

1 P-QB4	N-KB3
2 P-KN3	P-K3
3 B-N2	P-Q4
4 N-KB3	B-K2
5 P-Q4	0-0
6 QN-Q2	P-QN3
7 0-0	B-N2
8 PxP	

Varying from 8 P-N3 which Korchnoi played against Petrosian in their eleventh Candidates' game last year.

8 . . .	PxP
9 N-K5	QN-Q2
10 QN-B3	P-B4
11 P-N3	P-QR4

Korchnoi felt this was not good but I disagree. The weakening of Black's QN4 square never turns out to be important, while the threat of . . . P-QR5 hanging over White's head is very annoying.

12 B-N2	N-K5

13 R-B1

Korchnoi even considered 13 R-N1 here, which shows that he was perturbed by the possibility of . . . P-QR5.

13 . . .	R-K1
14 NxN?	

This prematurely reduces the tension. White should have kept things on the boil with 14 P-K3 though I doubt if he could then boast of any objective advantage.

14 . . .	QxN
15 N-K5	Q-K3
16 N-Q3	B-Q3
17 PxP	PxP

94

18 P-K3

White is slowly forfeiting the initiative. Black's hanging pawns on QB4 and Q4 control a lot of space and his development is more efficient.

White could not of course play 18 BxN QxB 19 NxP? because of 19 . . . BxN 20 RxB P-Q5 21 P-B3 Q-K6+ followed by 22 . . . P-Q6 winning.

18 . . .	P-R5
19 PxP	B-R3
20 R-K1	BxN?

White was faced by a number of tactical threats but this hasty decision releases most of them. Best was 20 . . . Q-B4 21 R-B2 B-B5 increasing the pressure.

| 21 QxB | RxP |
| 22 Q-N3 | |

Objectively White should have no difficulty in drawing now, but Korchnoi only had twenty minutes (against Karpov's fifty) in which to reach the time control at move 40.

| 22 . . . | R(R5)-R1 |
| 23 BxN | PxB |

20 . . . QxB 21 R(K1)-Q1 P-B5 leads to liquidation and an early draw. Karpov probably decided to chance his arm on Korchnoi's clock.

24 QxQ	RxQ
25 P-QR3	R-R5
26 KR-Q1	P-B3
27 K-B1?	

Better was 27 R-B3 followed by 28 R-N3 when White's active rooks leave him with nothing to fear.

| 27 . . . | K-B2 |
| 28 R-B2 | B-K2 |

| 29 R-Q7 | R-N3 |
| 30 P-N4 | |

A more dignified way of drawing was 30 RxP (threatening to double on the seventh) 30 . . . K-K1 31 R(B5)-B7 B-Q3 32 RxB RxR 33 RxP and White is slightly better, although he cannot win.

| 30 . . . | K-K3 |
| 31 R-B7 | R-R1 |

Now White's adventurous rook is in some danger but in trying to find a way to trap it Karpov also got into time trouble and I noticed that the world champion was becoming flustered.

| 32 R-Q2 | P-N3 |

32 . . . R-Q1 would have given White some problem.

| 33 K-N2 | P-B4 |
| 34 P-N5! | |

Now White has nothing to worry about. If necessary he can bale out with B-B6. Soon Karpov is reduced to trying to exchange the rook he wanted to trap.

34 . . .	R-Q3
35 R-B2	R(Q3)-R3
36 P-KR4	R-(R1)-R2
37 R-B8	R-R1
38 R-B7	R-(R1)-R2
39 R-B8	

Draw agreed

(Times: 2.26 — 2.27)

GAME TWENTY

At 10.45 on the morning of the twentieth game I was dragged out of bed by Camponanes and summoned to a meeting of the jury at which the future of the two Ananda Margas was discussed. I promised that they would watch the games in civilian clothes (i.e. without their saffron robes and turbans) and also that they would maintain a low profile by abandoning the lotus position. It was decided to leave the whole matter to Camponanes, who resolved only one hour before the game was due to start that the Ananda Margas would not be allowed to enter. I then explained to him that this decision was unfair and it was duly modified by providing that people with criminal records (no names mentioned!) should be banned from the auditorium as from game twenty-one. The Ananda Margas were allowed in for the last time to watch game twenty on condition they behaved normally.

Meanwhile Korchnoi had been receiving support from various interesting quarters. A telegram from France saying *"Avec nous en coeur"* purported to come from an eminent literary quartet Arrabal, Becket, Ionesco and Sartre. We were not sure whether it was genuine but we certainly hoped so. The backing of Fernando Arrabal, as originator of the *Theatre of Panic*, seemed especially appropriate!

Korchnoi also received a telegram from Donald Woods, whose outspoken criticisms of *apartheid* had caused him to be banned in South Africa and who now lives in England. His message was: "Have African witch doctor casting spells for you. Free world hopes for your victory." Was one of these spells resposible for Karpov's forty-second move in the twentieth game?

In game twenty Korchnoi defended with a line of the Caro Kann which I recently examined in *Modern Chess Theory*. Although it is unpopular I have a lot of faith in it and managed to convert Korchnoi. The opening was a surprise to Karpov and he was unable to obtain any real advantage. But in the middlegame Korchnoi faltered seriously, wasting time with inane knight manoeuvres, and eventually he allowed his queenside to collapse. At adjournment his position was hopeless but then a miracle occurred. Karpov had not sealed the obvious and immediately decisive move. Karpov should still have won but further mistakes allowed Kochnoi to escape with a totally unexpected draw.

After the game Korchnoi said: 'No amount of gurus will help me if I play bad moves". This sober admission I took as a good sign.

Karpov now led 4-1 with 15 draws.

White: Karpov
Black: Korchnoi

Caro Kann Defence

1 P-K4	P-QB3
2 P-Q4	P-Q4
3 N-Q2	PxP
4 NxP	N-B3
5 NxN+	KPxN

This move has often been condemned but the situation is deceptive and Golombek, Bronstein and Flohr have all used the move to good effect. White obtains the long-term advantage of a potential queenside pawn majority, but, despite the doubled KBP, Black's mass of kingside pawns offer good compensation, since the front KBP can advance while the rear KBP stays at home to shelter the Black king. As the game proceeds all these themes are illustrated.

6 B-QB4	N-Q2

Korchnoi's theoretical novelty. The idea is to save a tempo on such lines as 6 . . . B-Q3 7 Q-K2+ B-K2

7 N-K2	B-Q3
8 0-0	0-0

8 . . . Q-B2 is also possible

9 B-B4	N-N3
10 B-Q3	

An interesting decision. The natural move would be 10 B-QN3 to keep the bishop aimed at KB7 but Karpov appreciates that the bishop will ultimately be more useful on the KR1-QR8 diagonal supporting the advance of his queenside pawn majority.

10 . . .	B-K3
11 P-QB3	N-Q4
12 BxB	QxB
13 Q-Q2	QR-Q1

Keeping a watchful eye on the prospective passed pawn.

14 KR-K1	P-KN3
15 QR-Q1	K-N2
16 B-K4	N-B2
17 P-QN3	KR-K1
18 B-N1	

It looks strange to abandon the ideal diagonal but there were tactical threats against the bishop. If instead 18 B-B3 Korchnoi was planning the complicated manoeuvre 18 . . . P--R4 (threatening 19 . . . B-N5) 19 P-KR3 B-B1 followed by . . . N-K3 and . . . N-N4 molesting the bishop.

18 . . .	B-N5
19 P-KR3	BxN
20 RxB	RxR
21 QxR	N-Q4
22 Q-Q2	

22 . . .	N-B5?

Korchnoi's opening has been a success but now he throws away the fruits of his good play. After the obvious 22 . . . P-KB4 White's

97

bishop is deprived of any immediate possibility of returning to the key KR1-QR8 diagonal and Black could then manoeuvre his knight to K5 via KB3 or carry out a general advance of his kingside pawns in more favourable circumstances than later occurs in the game.

23 B-K4

Of course. Now Black has to struggle for survival.

23 ...   P-KB4

'Too late. Too late she cried, waving her wooden leg'.

24 B-B3   P-KR3
25 P-KR4

Planning to cut off the knight, which involves Black in a general retreat. Still the pawn on KR4 does become a target.

Also dangerous was 25 P-Q5 PxP 26 Q-Q4 with moves like QxRP and PxP in the offing.

Karpov had now spent one hour twenty-five minutes and Korchnoi one hour fifty minutes.

25 ...   N-K3
26 Q-K3   N-B2
27 P-B4   P-B5?

I believe this was a blunder overlooking White's 29th move. Correct was 27 . . . Q-B3

28 Q-B3   Q-B3
29 Q-R5

DIAGRAM

Exceedingly strong. Korchnoi's now used up fifteen of his remaining thirty-five minutes, but then proceeded to move at blitz speed. Since 29 Q-R5 wipes out Black's queen side the situation is fast becoming critical for Korchnoi.

29 ...   N-K3

30 P-Q5   PxP
31 PxP   P-N3

Not 31 . . . N-Q5? 32 RxN.

32 Q-R4

A powerful *intermezzo* again preventing . . . N-Q5.

32 ...   N-B4
33 QxRP   N-Q2
34 P-Q6   QxRP
35 Q-B7   Q-B3
36 P-QN4   P-R4

A last desperate attempt to exploit his kingside majority with a rush of his peasant army.

37 P-R4   K-R3
38 P-N5

Of course 38 P-R5 was also possible but I suppose Karpov did not want to eliminate the weak Black QNP.

38 ...   P-N4
39 B-B6   N-B4
40 P-Q7   K-N2

40 . . . N-K3 at once would have saved a tempo.

41 R-K1   N-K3

DIAGRAM

42 Q-Q6??

The disastrous sealed move over which Karpov thought for thirty minutes. After the expected 42 QxNP Black's kingside counterplay

soon fizzles out e.g. 42 . . . P-N5
43 P-R5 P-N6 44 PxP PxP 45
Q-K3 Q-R5 46 R-Q1 and Black
can do nothing. 43 . . . P-B6 is a
better chance but it is still extremely forlorn.

Our analysis lasted through the
night but it was haunted by the
knowledge that 42 QxP was
murderous. Murei did not even
dare to watch the resumption of
play since he could not bear to
face the prospect of 42 QxP being
played. There were sighs of relief
all round from the rats who had
not left the sinking ship when the
queen appeared on Q6 not QN6.

42 . . .	P-N5
43 K-B1	

A typical Karpov safety precau-
tion. If 43 R-K5 P-N6 44 P-R5
PxRP 45 P-N6 P-B6! exploiting
the theme of Black's opening
variation in a particularly striking
way e.g. 46 PxNP PxP 47 BxP
RxP 48 QxR QxR and Black can
hold on since the White king is
exposed. Or 46 PxBP Q-R5 47
PxP QxP+ and again Black will
probably obtain a perpetual. Finally 46 BxP allows 46 . . . PxP+
47 KxP RxP etc.

43 . . .	P-N6?

Overcome with relief Korchnoi

moved too hastily. 43 . . . P-R5
would have saved an important
tempo.

44 Q-K5	P-R5
45 P-R5	

This pawn sacrifice keeps White's
chances alive.

45 . . .	PxP
46 P-N6	QxQ
47 RxQ	R-QN1
48 P-N7	N-Q1

Black's only chance is a last-ditch
Nimzowitschian blockade. His
pieces are now spectacularly paralysed.

After the game Murei commented
that Black's position was now
reminiscent of Korchnoi's situation during the Nazi blockade of
Lenningrad.

49 R-K8	K-B3

Of course 49 . . . NxB loses to 50
PxR NxR 51 P-Q8=Q.

50 PxP	BPxP
51 K-K2	K-N2
52 B-B3?	

This allows the Black QRP to become a menace and White has to
suspend his grip. Correct was the
manoeuvre 52 K-B3 P-B4 53 B-R4
followed by 54 B-B2 and 55 BxP
which should win for White.

52 . . .	P-R5
53 R-K4	

If 53 K-Q3 P-B4 54 K-B3 P-B5
55 K-N4 RxP+ 56 BxR NxB and
Black should not lose.

53 . . .	K-B3
54 RxQRP	K-K2
55 RxP	

If 55 R-R8 RxP 56 BxR NxB
draws. White cannot win the exchange ahead if Black can pick up
White's QP and retain his own

KBP and here he can achieve both objectives.

55 ...	KxP
56 R-KB4?	

The last chance was 56 R-R8. Now it is a draw.

56 ...	K-Q3
57 R-QN4	K-B2
58 R-B4+	K-Q2
59 B-N4+	K-K1
60 R-K4+	K-B1
61 B-Q7	RxP

Not 61 ... NxP? allowing the pin 62 R-QN4 followed by 63 B-B6.

62 R-K8+	K-N2
63 RxN	R-N7+

DIAGRAM

Draw agreed.

White must defend his last pawn by 64 K-B3 but then Black draws

by the pin 64 ... R-Q7 with the unanswerable threat of 65 ... K-B3 and 66 ... K-K2

A difficult, fascinating but flawed game.

(Times: 3.29 — 3.35)

Note these are the times after move 60. No official record exists of the times at the end of the game.

GAME TWENTY-ONE

12th and 13th September

In accordance with Camponanes' edict the Anada Margas absented themselves from the Playing Hall and it looked as though the match might be
about to enter a sane phase. But students of sensation need not worry.
Our mystical friends will shortly return to enliven these pages!

The twenty-first game featured a great come-back by Korchnoi. He
reverted to the variation of the Queen's Gambit Declined he had played
in the ninth game — partly out of devilry since Tal had written in *64* that
the variation was harmless . The Russians had a startling innovation ready
which most observers assumed had been fed to Karpov by his more risk-
prone seconds Tal and Zaitsev. Korchnoi calmly demonstrated that
Black's violence was premature and emerged from the complications
with an extra pawn. Careless play allowed Karpov to regain the pawn but
then the champion returned the favour and allowed the challenger to
adjourn a pawn up. Although we started on the wrong track we even-
turally analysed the adjourned position more efficently than the Russians.
The position was not clearly won for Korchnoi but it required more
accurate defence from Karpov than it received. After the champion fell
into a neat trap the challenger made no mistake and finished off with an
elegant piece sacrifice.

After the game Korchnoi commented to the assembled press "Lord
forgive them. They know not what they do." This was presumably a
reference to the Russians' adjournment analysis which for the first time
was substantially inferior to our own — an encouraging sign.

Despite mistakes on both sides this game was generally considered the
best of the match so far. Both players played creatively and it was the
first decisive game in which the result could be attributed more to good
play by the winner than unforced errors by the loser.

Karpov remained hot favourite but this game made it clear that Korchnoi
was not going to surrender without a fight, as many had feared after his
debacle in the seventeenth game.

Karpov now led 4-2 with 15 draws.

White: Korchnoi	1 P-QB4	N-KB3
Black: Karpov	2 N-QB3	P-K3
	3 N-B3	P-Q4
Queen's Gambit Declined	4 P-Q4	B-K2

5 B-B4	0-0
6 P-K3	P-B4
7 QPxP	BxP
8 Q-B2	N-B3
9 R-Q1	Q-R4
10 P-QR3	

All so far as in the ninth game.

10 ...	R-K1

A new move, varying from 10 ... B-K2 played in the ninth game.

11 N-Q2	P-K4
12 B-N5	

12 ...	N-Q5

The point of Black's tenth move. Although the move came as a terrible shock, analysis convinced Korchnoi that the positon did not justify such violence and he fell back in good Steinitzian order.

13 Q-N1

Karpov now stopped moving instantaneously and the Russians trooped off to the press room to analyse. Since Karpov's innovation turns out badly the Russian prepared analysis must have overlooked something but can it really have been this natural retreat? Korchnoi is renowned for grabbing material and trying to weather the ensuing storm but, as in the tenth game, he now decides that discretion is the better part of valour. His caution was justified e.g. (A) 13 PxN PxP+ 14 N-K2 N-N5 (threatening 15 . . . P-Q6 and 16 . . . BxP mate) 15 B-R4 PxP 16 QxP N-K4 with . . . P-Q6 and . . . N-Q6 in the offing. (B) 13 PxN PxP+ 15 B—K2 PxN 16 N-N3 Q-N3 17 NxB QxN 18 BxN PxB does not accomphish anything for White.

13 ...	B-B4

If 13 . . . B-KN5 14 BxN PxB 15 NxP! BxR 16 KxB leaves Black exposed to a multitude of threats such as 16 P-QN4, 16 PxN and 16 NxP+.

14 B-Q3	P-K5
15 B-B2	

15 BxN PxB(Q6) 16 BxN BxB 17 NxP P-QN4 is unclear. It is possible that the cynical 15 B-B1 would have refuted Black's conception entirely, but Korchnoi feared this might be going slightly too far on the Steinitzian path.

The text has the disadvantage that it allows Black to exchange his errant knight but at least Black's centre remains a target for Korchnoi to tilt at.

15 ...	NxB+
16 QxN	Q-R3

If 16 . . . PxP, 17 BxN PxB 18 P-QN4 PxP e.p. 19 NxP QxP 20 R-R1 Q-N5 21 R-R4 Q-N3 22 N-Q5 looks good for White and so Karpov decides to sacrifice a pawn for reasonable counterplay.

17 BxN	QxB
18 N-N3	B-Q3
19 RxP	R-K4
20 N-Q4	R-QB1

DIAGRAM

21 RxR?

A careless move which loses the extra pawn. Correct was 21 NxB.

21 ...	QxR
22 NxB	QxN(B4)
23 0-0	RxP
24 R-Q1	Q-K4?

A plausible blunder which Karpov played after only a few minutes thought. Best was 24 ... B-K2 25 Q-N3 Q-B1 and Black has little to fear.

25 P-KN3	P-QR3
26 Q-N3	P-QN4
27 P-QR4	

Now Black cannot satisfactorily defend his queenside. Karpov finds the best chance but it is not very impressive.

27 ...	R-N5
28 Q-Q5	QxQ
29 RxQ	B-B1
30 PxP	P-QR4
31 R-Q8	RxP(N7)
32 R-R8	P-B4
33 RxP	B-N5
34 R-R8+	K-B2
35 N-R4	R-N8+
36 K-N2	B-Q3
37 R-R7+	K-B3
38 P-N6	B-N1
39 R-R8	

Panno pointed out the ingenious

39 R-B7! threatening 40 R-B8. Black cannot then play 39 ... BxR 40 PxB R-B8 41 N-N6 RxP 42 N-Q5+ or 39 ... R-N5 40 N-B5 RxP 41 N-Q7+ K-N3 42 R-B8 winning.

39 ...	B-K4
40 N-B5	B-Q3
41 P-N7	K-K2
42 R-KN8	B-K4

43 P-B4

The sealed move which is White's only way of making progress. The point is to free White's king and open up Q3 for the knight.

43 ...	PxP e.p. +
44 KxP	K-B2
45 R-B8	

We had analysed the adjoined position until the last hour. We wasted a lot of time considering the unnecessary piece sacrifice 45 R-Q8 K-K2 46 R-Q7+ K-K1 47 P-K4 R-N4 48 PxP RxN 49 RxP but we finally decided that 49 ... P-R3! refutes the whole idea since White needs KN5 for his rook while rook endings with an extra pawn are drawn. An hour before the second session Korchnoi abandoned the whole unsound idea and we frantically started analysing the text move.

45 . . .	K-K2
46 P-R3!	

A subtle trap which the Russians overlooked.

46 . . .	P-R4?

Correct was 46 . . . R-N4 when White still has chances but there is no clear win. After the text all Black's pawns are exposed along the fourth rank.

47 R-KN8	K-B2
48 R-Q8	P-N4

The point of the trap is that the intended 48 . . . K-K2 loses to 49 R-Q7+ K-K1 50 R-Q5 B-B3 51 RxP since Black's KRP is attached and so he has no time to pick up White's QNP.

49 P-N4!

A very good move. 49 N-Q7 wins a piece but probably not the game after 49 . . . P-N5+ 50 PxP RPxP+ 51 K-K2 BxP.

49 N-Q3 also only draws after 49 . . . P-N5+ 50 PxP RPxP+ 51 K-B2 K-K2 52 NxB KxR 53 P-N8=Q+ RxQ 54 N-B6+ K-B2 55 NxR KxN 56 P-K4 K-B2!.

49 . . .	RPxP+
50 PxP	K-K2
51 R-KN8	PxP+

If now 51 . . . B-Q3 52 N-R6 RxP 53 R-N7+ wins.

52 KxP	K-B2
53 R-B8	B-Q3
54 P-K4	

Not at once 54 KxP BxN 55 P-N8=Q RxQ 56 RxR BxP+ winning White's last pawn and leaving a drawn R v B ending. But now 55 KxP is a threat.

54 . . .	R-N8+
55 K-B5	P-N5
56 P-K5	R-B8+
57 K-K4	R-K8+
58 K-Q5	R-Q8+

If 58 . . . BxP 59 N-Q3 wins.

59 N-Q3!

An elegant piece sacrifice with which to round off the game.

59 . . .	RxN+
60 K-B4	

Schmid was now hovering with a White queen ready for the expected promotion of White's QNP. Korchnoi skittishly requested that he have a rook knight and bishop ready as well in case he decided to underpromote. **Karpov** took the hint and **resigned** to the accompaniment of loud cheers and chapping.

A fascinating, difficult but flawed game.

(Times: 3.39 —3.31)

GAME TWENTY-TWO

14th and 15th September

After the Ananda Margas first appeared on the scene Camponanes ordered a summary of their trial and before the twenty-second game he distributed the fruits of his research. The report on the trial proved to be a very damning document which put both the individuals, Dwyer and Shepperd, the the Ananda Marga organisation as a whole in a very bad light.

The report filed by provincial fiscal B. Jose Castillo stated that in the case of The People of The Philippines vs. Steven Michael Dwyer and Victoria Shepperd (Seventh Judicial District of the Circuit Criminal Court) the accused had been convicted of the fustrated murder of an Indian Embassy official, Jyoti Suarap Vaid in February 1978 in Makati Metro Manila. The summary of the trial appears to be full of inconsistencies and even accuses Ananda Marga of being communist inspired! Rather oddly for a legal document it contains a general condemnation of Ananda Marga which I quote:

> "The fact that the Ananda Marga does not stop at anything to achieve its diabolical ends unmistakably makes its followers not only threats to individual lives but also to national security. The symptom and the warning on this particular occasion had surfaced: the Ananda Marga considers government officials as fair game in their missions of assassination."

Whether or not the Ananda Margas were rightly convicted, it is not surprising that their association with the match gave rise to concern. The issues involved (especially the importance to be attached to the existence of a serious criminal charge before the truth of the charge has been finally determined) bore a striking similarity to those which were simultaneously dogging the Liberal Party Conference in England.

The day the report of the trial was released there was an exchange of letters between Lim Kok Ann and Camponanes extracts from which follow. (Italics mine).

Lim Kok Ann to Camponanes
"I hope I am not being alarmist but I cannot help being concerned by the intrusion of the Ananda Marga people into our proceedings. Although it has been reported that the members of

the sect are not authorised to undertake acts of violence by their leader it is also reported that such acts have been performed, e.g. suicide by burning in the name of love for all humanity. I hardly need point out that all manner of atrocities have been performed in the same name in human history down the ages."

. . . . .

"I am sorry to trouble you with these groundless fears, perhaps, and *I am sure you will take care of the matter* in the appropriate manner."

Camponanes to Lim Kok Ann

"[The Ananda Margas'] continued association with its implications and consequences will compel us to ask for a technical recess of the match *until this question is resolved by the jury.* This failing, we are left with no alternative but to terminate the match for reasons of general and personal security."

So once again the match was in danger of ending prematurely and the Chairman of the Jury and the Match Organiser were each hoping the other would do something about it. The Korchnoi camp had already conceded one point when we acquiesced in the decision that the Ananda Margas should not enter the Playing Hall itself. We now made another concession by persuading the Ananda Margas to move from the Pines Hotel to the private villa which had been supplied for Korchnoi's use during the match. The agreement that their activities should in future be confined to consenting yogis in private assuaged the fears of the organisers and the match was on again. A few days later the dismissal of the Ananda Margas to the shadows was confirmed by my announcement that they should no longer be considered part of the Korchnoi delegation.

Having quoted the views of so many other people, I had better express my own views on the Ananda Margas. Perched firmly on my fence all I can say is that it is possible they were a genuine security risk. It is also possible that they were framed and the whole issue blown up out of all proportion. It is possible they were basically publicity seekers for their own cause. It is also possible that they were good hearted people who just wanted to help Korchnoi. It is almost impossible to decide.

The Ananda Marga dispute was merely concerned with their public manifestation. Although personally I did not find some of their antics exactly to my taste, I cannot deny that in their private capacity they appeared to be helpful to Korchnoi. He had appeared much calmer since his return from Manila where he met the Ananda Margas in the interval between the seventeenth and eighteenth games. It is true that his recovery could also be attributed to the settlement of the Zukhar dispute at the same time but I think it would be churlish to deny that, through the medium of their spiritual exercises, the Ananda Margas played an important part.

Returning at last to the chess, the twenty-second was in a way a disappointment for both players.

Korchnoi, playing the French Defence again, obtained an uncomfortable middlegame in which he was thoroughly outplayed by Karpov. It was clear that he had still not found a satisfactory defence with Black.

Karpov had even more reason to be disappointed. He wasted his earlier fine play by mistakes *after* the time control. When the game was adjourned on the forty-seventh move his opportunity had gone. In the second session Korchnoi secured a draw though it took some very accurate endgame play to do so. Karpov's disappointment must have been increased by the knowledge that his missed opportunity was so unnecessary. He could have made virtually certain of the win by sealing as soon as he reached the time control.

Golombek cited the game as evidence for the existence of life after death.

Karpov now led 4-2 with 16 draws.

White: Karpov
Black: Korchnoi

French Defence

1 P-K4	P-K3
2 P-Q4	P-Q4
3 N-Q2	P-QB4
4 KPxP	KPxP
5 B-N5+	B-Q2
6 Q-K2+	B-K2

Varying from 6 . . . Q-K2 played in the sixteenth game.

7 PxP	N-KB3
8 N-N3	0-0
9 B-K3	R-K1
10 N-B3	

An unusual move which Karpov played at blitz speed. Korchnoi, after long thought, now decides to regain the pawn with a pseudo-combination but White retains the initiative in the opposite bishops middle game.

10 . . .	BxP
11 NxB	Q-R4+
12 Q-Q2	QxB
13 0-0-0	P-QN3

Better was 13 . . . B-N5, to inflict counter-weaknesses on White's position.

14 NxB	QNxN
15 K-N1	N-K5
16 Q-Q3	QxQ
17 RxQ	N(Q2)-B3
18 P-KR3	

This is just the kind of position not to have against Karpov, who can develope his offensive against White's isolated queen pawn virtually unmolested.

18 . . .	N-B4
19 R(Q3)-Q1	N-K3

20 P-B3	P-QN4

In search of counterplay, Korchnoi exposes his pawns.

21 N-Q4	P-QR3
22 N-Q2	P-QR4
23 R-Q3	QR-N1
24 R(R1)-Q1	P-R3
25 P-KB4	QR-B1
26 P-KN4	

26 ...	P-Q5

Karpov has played with great skill and Black's position is now critical. Nobody could see an answer to White's projected P-KN5. Korchnoi solves (well - not quite solves) his problems by sacrificing the weakling QP to obtain good squares for his knights. This is an imaginative solution but not quite adequate.

26 ... P-Q5 is pure Nimzowitsch and the following quotation from *My System* could easily apply to it:

"So powerful is the pawn's desire to press on here to expand (of which fact indeed visible recognition is given in the way the officers, laying aside all pride of cast, picturesquely group themsleves round this simple foot soldier), that our pawn often seems ready to advance on his own account, when to do so will cost him his life — and now all of a sudden the forces in the rear come to life".

27 PxP	N-Q4
28 R-KB1	P-N5

Korchnoi opined that he would have sufficient compensation if his pawns were still on QR2 and QN3 — but they aren't.

29 B-Q2	R-K2
30 P-B5	

If 30 N-K3 N(K3)xP 31 RxN NxR 32 N-B5 R-K7 and the knight on KB5 is immune.

30 ...	N-N4
31 N-K3	N-B3
32 P-Q5	

Sensibly returning the sacrificed pawn in order to envigorate his own queen pawn and attack Black's queenside.

32 ...	NxRP

32 ... N(N4)-K5 offered better practical chances.

33 P-Q6	R-Q2
34 N-Q5	NxN
35 RxN	R-R1
36 B-K3	N-N4

In desperate time trouble Korchnoi misses the last real chance, which lay in 36 ... R-R3.

37 B-N6	N-K5
38 R(B1)-Q1	P-R5
39 R(Q5)-Q4	R-K1
40 RxP	RxP
41 RxR	NxR

DIAGRAM

42 B-B7??

Why on earth did not Karpov seal the simple 42 RxP? He had

plenty of time and was in any case already past the time control.

42 . . .	R-K8+
43 K-B2	N-K1
44 B-R5	P-R6
45 R-N8	R-K2
46 B-N4?	

46 PxP must be superior. Did he overlook that Black's next move or what??

46 . . .	R-K7+
47 K-Q3	PxP

The sealed move over which Korchnoi pondered for forty minutes. It later transpired that 47 . . . RxP 48 RxN+ K-R2 49 BxP RxP leads to a position where Black has time for . . . P-KB3, when the perpetual threat of . . . P-R4 means White cannot win. But who would dare seal a move like 47 . . . RxP?

On resumption — after many hours of analysis — we believed that Black could still draw, in spite of White's outside passed pawn supported by a bishop. The Russians had announced that 47 . . . RxP was a draw but that 47 . . . PxP lost but, as in the previous game, our adjournment analysis proved superior to theirs. It was Korchnoi who moved at

lightning speed in the second session while Karpov had to wrack his brains trying to find a win which wasn't there.

48 B-Q2

48 B-B3 P-N8=Q+ 49 RxQ RxP 50 R-N8 transposes into the drawn piece sacrifice line referred to in the previous note.

48 . . .	R-K2
49 P-R4	R-Q2+
50 K-B2	K-R2
51 RxP	P-R4!

Necessary, in order to create targets for the knight.

52 PxP	N-Q3
53 R-R2	

Another key variation is 53 R-N4 NxP 54 P-R5 N-Q5+ followed by . . . N-B3 and . . . NxP when White cannot win despite his extra piece.

53 . . .	NxP
54 P-R5	N-Q5+
55 K-B3	N-B3
56 P-R6	R-Q4

After this Karpov stopped for a long think. Black wipes out White's kingside and White cannot shift the knight on Black's QB3.

57 B-B4

57 P-R6 may be a better try but it doesn't work either.

57 . . .	R-B4
58 B-Q6	R-Q4
59 B-N3	R-KN4
60 B-B2	RxP
61 K-B4	N-R4+
62 K-B3	N-B3
63 R-R4	K-N1

This move, over which Korchnoi thought for half an hour draws, since White cannot prevent the Black king reaching Q2 and defending the knight on QB3. Karpov now resigns himself to the draw.

64 K-B4   **N-R4+**
Draw agreed.

(Times: 3.34 — 4.00)

GAME TWENTY-THREE

16th September

Korchnoi's villa had now turned into a mystics playground with gurus levitating in and out at will. Some even levitated into my room which meant I had to move to the Pines Hotel permanently.

One group of gurus was of course the celebrated Ananda Margas, who now had nowhere else to go, poor things, having been banished from both the Playing Hall and the Pines Hotel. The other group comprised the parapsychological posse of Father Bulatao's decorous disciples who were free to roam at will — and did so. They were now led by one Lun, a Belgian.

I was having coffee with Ms. Leeuwerik one day when the phone rang and a waiter informed her that a Mr. Rasputin wanted to speak to her. I managed to maintain a stiff upper lip at this startling intelligence and merely uttered a silent prayer that Korchnoi and Ms. Leeuwerik would not suffer from the Red Army the fate which befell two earlier adherents of the mad monk, Nicholas and Alexandra. I was reassured when Ms. Leeuwerik explained that Rasputin was merely the code name for the aforementioned Lun. I do not think he really deserves such an illustrious sobriquet and would tentatively suggest as an alternative "The Wild Bore".

The twenty-third game was a high-class encounter, though not a particularly sensational one. Korchnoi quietly built up an advantage but Karpov defended skilfully and the game petered out into a draw shortly before the end of the first session.

The draw was accomplished in yet another new manner. Korchnoi simply wrote ½-½ and signed his score sheet and waited for Karpov to do likewise. An interesting situation would have arisen if Karpov had declined to do so!

Karpov now led 4-2 with 17 draws.

White: Korchnoi			
Black: Karpov		4 P-Q4	B-K2
		5 B-B4	0-0
		6 P-K3	P-B4
Queen's Gambit Declined		7 QPxP	BxP
		8 Q-B2	N-B3
1 P-QB4	N-KB3	9 R-Q1	Q-R4
2 N-QB3	P-K3	10 P-QR3	B-K2
3 N-B3	P-Q4		

Karpov abandons the line 10 . . . R-K1 11 N-Q2 P-K4 12 B-N5 N-Q5 which was a glorious failure in the twenty-first game.

11 N-Q2	P-K4
12 B-N5	P-Q5
13 N-N3	Q-N3

Karpov's improvement on 13 . . . Q-Q1 played in the ninth game. We had analysed it in some detail and concluded that White could maintain a slight edge.

14 BxN	BxB
15 N-Q5	Q-Q1
16 B-Q3	P-KN3

Considerably better than 16 . . . P-KR3 when the weakening of the White squares means that White can retain his knight on Q5. The text also threatens 17 . . . B-N2.

17 PxP	NxP
18 NxN	PxN
19 NxB+	QxN
20 0-0	

The position is simplified, but White has some advantage based on the mobility of his queenside pawns. Objectively, though, Black's QP should always hold the balance.

| 20 . . . | B-K3 |
| 21 KR-K1 | |

More promising is 21 P-B4 B-B4 22 BxB PxB 23 Q-N3 entertaining such ideas as Q-N3+ followed by Q-N5. After the game Korchnoi described 21 P-B4 as "not the sort of move I play", but what about the third game of this match?

| 21 . . . | QR-B1 |
| 22 P-QN3 | |

Korchnoi consolidates his position. It was also possible to try to molest Black's queenside by 22 Q-R4.

22 . . .	KR-Q1
23 B-K4	R-B2
24 Q-Q2	B-N5
25 P-B3	

Although he had played the opening very quickly, Korchnoi only had forty-five minutes left after this move, while Karpov — incredibly — had only used about forty minutes thinking time. Anyway Korchnoi's thought now begins to bear fruit and he obtains a tangible initiative.

25 . . .	B-K3
26 P-QR4	P-N3
27 P-R5	P-QN4

Karpov could have played possum but he generally chose to become active when Korchnoi had less than an hour left on his clock.

| 28 PxP | BxP |
| 29 R-N1 | B-Q4 |

29 . . . R-B6 may be stronger.

| 30 P-N6 | PxP |
| 31 RxP | |

31 PxP is also dangerous for Black, but our investigations revealed that Black could still draw.

| 31 . . . | R-B3 |
| 32 RxR | |

It looks good to try 32 BxB RxB

33 R-K8+ K-N2 34 R(N6)-N8 but after 34 . . . Q-N4 it is White who has problems.

| 32 . . . | BxR |
| 33 B-Q3 | |

White still has some pull with his distant passed pawn but Karpov finds a clever manoeuvre to neutralise it. His . . . B-Q2 followed by . . . B-B4 is an excellent idea.

33 . . .	B-Q2
34 P-R6	B-B4
35 Q-B4	

I would prefer 35 R-R1, but Korchnoi has a neat tactical point in mind.

| 35 . . . | K-N2 |

36 BxB

Now the game burns out to a draw. Korchnoi had been planning 36 P-R7 BxB 37 Q-N8 B-B7 38 R-K8 winning but at the last minute he saw the brilliant counterstroke 37 . . . B-K7!! 38 RxB P-Q6 and Black draws e.g. 39 R-K8 Q-R8+.

36 . . .	QxB
37 QxQ	PxQ
38 R-R1	

Immediately after the game Korchnoi thought 38 K-B2 was a significant improvement, but it still leads to a draw.

38 . . .	P-Q6
39 K-B2	R-K1
40 R-R2	R-K2
41 R-Q2	R-K3
Draw agreed.	

After the game Korchnoi sat staring at the board for five minutes, unable to believe his position had not been winning at some stage.

(Times: 2.30 − 1.53)

GAME TWENTY-FOUR

19th September

Korchnoi prepared for the twenty-fourth game in a somewhat unconventional manner. The evening before the game an assortment of seeventeen parapsychologists, gurus, grandmasters and respectable girls and matrons assembled at Korchnoi's villa for a meditation session. Seated, of course, in the lotus position and forming a mystic circle we proceeded to chant the universal mantra *baba nam ke walam* for twenty minutes. After this spiritual cleansing our bodies were refreshed by a delicious meal of holy fruits and vegetables (meat being taboo to the Ananda Margas). Ananda Marga means 'Path of Bliss' and it now seemed to be living up to its name.

Korchnoi was so uplifted by this experience that he treated us to a spirited rendition of 'There's a Tavern in the Town' in Russian.

Whatever other effects this occasion had on Korchnoi's morale it must at least have made up for his cold, which he attributed to following the Ananda Margas' advice by sprinkling cold water on his eyes to soothe his nerves.

Korchnoi appeared to be in a daredevil mood in the twenty-fourth since he again defended with the Open Ruy Lopez which he had abandonned (for good reason) earlier in the match. Karpov seemed puzzled by the choice of opening, which was in fact largely bluff. He missed two opportunities of testing the soundness of Korchnoi's opening and drifted into an inferior middle game as a result of too automatic play. But Korchnoi was by then short of time and rejected the most forceful continuation (which he saw) in favour of one that led to a slight endgame advantage. Thereafter Karpov had no difficulty in defending and, although the game was adjourned, the second session was a formality. A draw was agreed after only four more moves.

Karpov now led 4-2 with 18 draws.

White: Karpov
Black: Korchnoi

Ruy Lopez

1 P-K4	P-K4
2 N-KB3	N-QB3
3 B-N5	P-QR3
4 B-R4	N-B3
5 0-0	NxP
6 P-Q4	P-QN4
7 B-N3	P-Q4
8 PxP	B-K3
9 P-B3	B-K2

Varying from 9 . . . B-QB4 played in earlier games.

10 B-B2	N-B4

114

11 P-KR3

Karpov spent fifteen minutes on this move but it is not the best. More dangerous for Black is the pawn sacrifice 11 N-Q4 (a common motif in this variation — compare game eight) 11 ... NxP 12 P-KB4 persecuting Black's minor pieces.

11 ...	0-0
12 R-K1	

Again 12 N-Q4 NxP 13 P-KB4 was unpleasant for Black. Korchnoi was even considering the humble 12 ... Q-Q2 in reply.

12 ...	Q-Q2
13 N-Q4	NxN
14 PxN	N-N2
15 N-Q2	

Rather tame. Why not 15 N-B3 P-QB4 16 PxP NxP 17 B-K3 planning 18 B-Q4?

15 ...	P-QB4
16 PxP	NxP
17 N-B3	B-B4

This clears up most of Black's problems. Of course White cannot accept the pawn e.g. 18 BxB QxB 19 QxP KR-Q1 20 Q-B6 QR-B1 21 Q-N6 N-Q6 22 R-B1 NxBP 23 RxN R-Q8+ etc

18 B-K3	QR-B1
19 R-QB1	BxB

20 RxB	N-K3
21 R-Q2	KR-Q1
22 Q-N3?	

This weak move hands over the initiative to Black. 22 B-N6 B-N5 achieves nothing but 22 R-Q3 keeps up a little pressure. Now White's queen is pushed out of play.

22 ...	R-B5

Bold but strong.

23 R(K1)-Q1	Q-N2
24 P-R3	P-N3

Korchnoi now only had about half an hour left and he was moving with excruciating slowness. He was considering here 24 ... P-R3 with the positional threat 25 ... B-N4 but he did not want to weaken his KB4. Nevertheless 24 ... P-R3 has probably the best move.

25 Q-R2	

This indicates the bankruptcy of White's middlegame strategy and suggests that the blind piling up on Black's QP was insufficently subtle. The queen can do nothing from this remote square but White had to try to regroup somehow.

25 ...	P-QR4
26 P-QN3	R-B6
27 P-QR4	

27 ...   PxP

Objectively the best move is 27 . . . P-N5 e.g. 28 B-Q4? RxN! 29 PxR B-N4 30 B-K3 P-Q5 and White's position collapses. Korchnoi saw this variation but, with only twenty minutes left on his clock, opted for a slightly advantageous endgame rather than a complicated middlegame — an understandable decision.

28 PxP

Not 28 QxP? RxP 29 QxP R-R1 trapping the queen.

28 ...   R-B5

28 . . . R-R6 29 Q-B2 R-QB1 30 Q-N1 also results in the exchange of Black's QP for Whites QRP.

29 R-Q3	K-N2
30 Q-Q2	RxP
31 B-R6+	K-N1
32 RxP	RxR
33 QxR	QxQ
34 RxQ	B-B1
35 BxB	KxB

Black's outside passed pawn merely constitutes a nominal advantage. White has no difficulty in drawing.

36 P-N3	K-K2
37 R-N5	N-B2
38 R-B5	N-K3
39 R-N5	N-Q1
40 K-N2	P-R3
41 N-Q2	R-R8
42 N-B4	

The sealed move. The second session only lasted about five minutes.

42 ...	N-B3
43 R-B5	K-Q2
44 N-N6+	K-B2
45 N-B8	KxN

The players now looked at each other with a mild surmise and **agreed a draw** — silent, upon a peak in Baguio.

(Times: 2.23 — 2.49)

116

GAME TWENTY-FIVE

23rd and 24th September

Dr Max Euwe, FIDE President, arrived in Baguio after the twenty-fourth game — just in time to witness another row blow up over the Ananda Margas.

I was summoned to a meeting of the jury at which the Chairman Lim Kok Ann read out a letter complaining that he had seen two members of the Ananda Marga in the lobby of the Pines Hotel and stating: "In my opinion this negates the undertaking given by Mr Keene." I was very annoyed for various reasons.

1. It was simply not true that the presence of the Ananda Margas in the Pines Lobby negated any undertaking I had given. I had said that the Ananda Margas would move from the Pines to Korchnoi's villa and this they had done. I had not said that they would not *visit* the Pines Hotel in their capacity as friends of Korchnoi who was resident at the hotel.

2. It seemed to be assumed that, as head of the Korchnoi delegation, I was in a position to direct the movements of the Ananda Margas. There *might* have been something in this if they had remained official members of the Korchnoi delegation with the various rights and obligations that status entailed. But, at the insistence of the organisers and much against Korchnoi's will, it had been agreed they should not be members of the delegation. So how could I or anyone else direct the movement of private individuals in a free country?

3. The complaint came not from the Russian delegation or the organisers but from the chairman of the jury. I have been brought up in a system in which the roles of judge and prosecutor are not combined and I believe this to be the best system. I was disappointed in Lim Kok Ann whom I have always regarded as a pillar of wisdom and good sense. On this occasion it appeared to be a case of "The Chairman doth protest too much".

4. Although I knew roughly what was in the offing I was not given an advance copy of Lim Kok Ann's letter (as the letter itself indicated) and the meeting was summoned at too short notice for me to prepare my defence properly.

Having had time to collect my thoughts, I have presented my case in (I hope) a dispassionate and cogent manner. But at the time I was simply furious and left the meeting in case I exploded. The meeting continued in my absence and reached no conclusions. The following day I wrote to Campomanes explaining my position as outlined above.

The matter was then allowed to drop. A few days later Lim Kok Ann offered an olive branch which I was happy to accept. We are now again good friends.

Perhaps I have devoted too much space to a petty incident which in the end led nowhere. But it does illustrate the trivia which in this match so often diverted attention from the chess and wasted everyone's time and nervous energy.

With the twenty-fifth game the match moved into extra time. All other world championship matches since the Second World War have been limited to twenty-four games and under the old rules Karpov would by now have won the match. As it was he was no nearer winning than he had been three weeks before when he scored his fourth victory in the seventeenth game.

The two contestants did not agree on many things during the match and the rule governing its duration was not one of them. Karpov disliked the open-ended system because, he said, he preferred to play for draws when in the lead, rather than have to try to increase his lead. Korchnoi favoured the new system for precisely that reason. He also said he believed he was better prepared for a long match (despite his age) and that Karpov was only programmed for a twenty-four game series.

My own view was that the open-ended system was fairer even though it did place an excessive premium on stamina. But the fact that nobody knew when the match would end was very inconvenient for all those connected with the match, especially for the organisers who were in effect required to write out a blank cheque for hotel bills etc.

Each player was entitled to three postponements before the twenty-fifth game. Korchnoi had already used all his and Karpov now claimed his third postponement. From now on each player was entitled to one more postponement for each additional eight games.

The twenty-fifth game was a dramatic encounter. Karpov gradually outplayed Korchnoi with Black but just before the time control he overlooked a tactical *coup*. Korchnoi displayed superb opportunism in playing the combination at all, with only seconds left on his clock, but he almost spoilt his chance by playing the moves of the combination in the wrong order. However, Karpov failed to exploit this slip. Once again his error came *after* the time control. Korchnoi adjourned with some advantage but although the game lasted until move eighty the draw was never in real doubt.

This was another lucky escape for Korchnoi. Stean likened his desperate combination to the act of a drunk jumping out of a plane with something strapped to his back, not sure whether it was a parachute or a rucksack. Fortunately it turned out to be a parachute.

Karpov now led 4-2 with 19 draws.

White Korchnoi   **English Opening**
Black: Karpov

1 P-QB4   N-KB3

2 N-QB3   P-K4

For the first time Karpov varies from his solid 2...P-K3 set up. Presumably he was dissatisfied with the positions he had been obtaining defending the Queen's Gambit.

3 P-KN3   B-N5
4 Q-N3

An unusual move which puzzled Karpov, who handled the opening slowly.

4 . . .   N-B3

Another idea was 4 . . . BxN 5QxB N-B3 planning ...P-Q4 to hound White's queen.

5 N-Q5

Avoiding ...BxN. Any capture of the knight now will grant White pressure on the QB file.

5 . . .   B-B4
6 P-K3

White adopts a Stauntonesque formation!

6 . . .   0-0
7 B-N2   NxN
8 PxN   N-K2
9 N-K2   P-Q3

Korchnoi considered the immediate 9...P-QB3 superior.

10 0-0   P-QB3
11 P-Q4   KPxP
12 KPxP   B-N3
13 B-N5   B-Q2
14 P-QR4

Up to now Korchnoi had moved quickly (having used half an hour against Karpov's hour), but he used forty minutes over this move and seemed to be losing the thread. The plan of driving back Black's KB is a good one but why spend forty minutes on it?

14 . . .   P-KR3
15 BxN   QxB
16 B-B3

A curious move. Better was 16KR-K1 or 16P-R5 QxN 17 PxB RPxP 18 QxP Q-N4 when the position is drawn since White's KB is not participating in the struggle.

16 . . .   QR-N1
17 P-R5   B-B2
18 Q-B3

Better was 18 KR-B1

18 . . .   KR-B1

19 N-B4?

White should have baled out with 19 P-R6 leading to a drawish position after 19...B-N3. 20 RPxP RxP 21 PxP BxP 22 BxB R(N2)-B2 threatening the bishop on QB3 and the knight on K7.

19 . . .   B-Q1
20 KR-K1   Q-B1

Karpov's subtle defence gradually gains him the upper hand. Soon White starts a full scale retreat.

21 Q-N3   B-N4
22 N-K2

Korchnoi thought for fifteen minutes over this move, leaving himself with only fourteen minutes for eighteen moves — horrendous time trouble.

22 . . .	B-B3
23 QR-Q1	P-B4
24 B-K4	Q-Q1
25 Q-R2	B-N5

Now White is strategically busted. The position resembles a Modern Benoni in which everything has gone wrong for White.

26 PxP	RxP
27 P-N4	R-B2
28 Q-N3	QR-B1
29 P-B3	B-Q2
30 Q-K3	P-R3
31 B-Q3	B-N7
32 K-N2	

Korchnoi does his best to patch together the tattered shreds of his position, but the following spectacular bishop invasion should have been decisive.

32 . . .	Q-B3
33 R-QN1	B-R5
34 N-B4	P-KN3
35 R-K2	B-B8
36 Q-K4	K-B1

Black could have won White's queen for rook and bishop by 36...R-K1. The resulting position would have been technically won for Black, though difficult. Could Karpov really have overlooked this, or was he playing for more?

| 37 P-N5 | PxP |
| 38 Q-N4 | R-B4?? |

Karpov overlooks a brilliant tactical point. The simple 38...BxN would have left White positionally crushed.

DIAGRAM
39 RxB?

With only seconds on his clock Korchnoi sees the right idea but gets the moves in the wrong order. Correct was the immediate

39 NxP+ when Black must accept the sacrifice and after 39...PxN 40 RxB RxR 41 R-K6 Q-N4 42 QxP+ K-N2 43 Q-Q7+ K-B1 44 Q-Q6+ leads to perpetual check.

| 39 . . . | RxR |
| 40 NxP+! | K-N2! |

Now Black does not have to accept the knight.

41 N-K7   R(B1)-B5?

After 41...R-Q1 Black would still have had winning chances.

42 BxR

The sealed move 42 QxQP was also possible but it does not make much difference. White now stands better but analysis convinced us that he could not win against the most accurate defence.

42 . . .   RxB

If 42...B-Q8 43 N-B5+ K-B1 44 Q-N2 QxQ 45 RxQ BxR 46 P-R6 wins for White.

43 QxQP

43 Q-N1 fails to 43...P-N5 44 N-B5+ K-R1 45 N-K3 Q-K4 46 Q-K1 (or 46 K-B2 Q-Q5) R-B6 47 N-Q1 R-B7. The text wins a pawn but the position remains an easy draw.

43 . . .   R-B6

A good move which obliges White to weaken himself with 44 P-B4, after which White has no winning chances.

44 P-B4	QxQ
45 N-B5+	K-N3
46 NxQ	B-N6
47 P-B5+	K-N2
48 N-K8+	K-B1
49 N-B6	K-N2
50 N-R5+	K-B1
51 N-B4	B-B5
52 R-K5	R-R6
53 P-Q6	R-R7+
54 K-B3	R-Q7
55 R-K7	RxQP
56 RxNP	R-R3
57 R-N6	RxP
58 RxRP	P-N5
59 R-QB6	B-N4
60 R-B1	P-N6
61 R-QN1	B-B5
62 K-K4	R-R7
63 K-Q4	R-QB7
64 N-Q3	BxN
65 KxB	RxP
66 RxP	

The position is now a book draw but, unperturbed by snoring from the audience, Korchnoi plays on for another fourteen moves before bowing to the inevitable.

I was interested to learn that on BBC television Bill Hartston (the learned author of *How to Cheat at Chess*) was asked whether one should make one's opponents suffer by playing on in positions such as this. He replied with an emphatic "Yes".

66 ...	K-N2
67 K-K4	R-R7
68 K-B4	R-R5+
69 K-N5	R-R4
70 P-N4	R-B4
71 K-R5	R-R4
72 R-KB3	R-N4
73 P-N5	R-N8
74 P-B6+	K-R2
75 R-KR3	R-KN8
76 R-R2	R-N6
77 R-R1	R-N7
78 R-R1	R-R7+
79 K-N4	K-N3
80 R-R8	R-N7+

Now, at last, a **draw** was agreed.

(Time: 5.17 — 3.27)

GAME TWENTY-SIX

26th September

Karpov had apparently been sleeping badly of late and he briefly moved from the Terraces Plaza Hotel to the Baguio Country Club and back again. He was certainly looking tired during the twenty-sixth game and this may explain his choice of the English Opening. He sometimes chooses this opening when he needs a rest. The only other occasion he had played this opening was in the sixth game which was played in the interval between the second and third sessions of the marathon fifth game.

Korchnoi defended with an inferior variation against the English. His excuse was that he did not want to give anything away when confronted by his own favourite opening. Karpov failed to capitalize on his opening advantage and Korchnoi found a neat way of forcing a drawn ending.

Karpov now led 4-2 with 20 draws.

White: Karpov
Black: Korchnoi

English Opening

1 P-QB4	P-K4
2 N-QB3	P-Q3
3 P-KN3	P-KB4
4 B-N2	N-QB3
5 P-Q3	N-B3
6 P-K3	B-K2
7 KN-K2	0-0
8 0-0	Q-K1
9 P-B4	B-Q1
10 P-QR3	R-N1
11 P-QN4	B-K3
12 N-Q5	P-QN4

Black has played an inferior defence to the English Opening. The risky text move was prompted by the knowledge that with normal methods Black stood badly.

13 B-N2	NPxP
14 QPxP	P-K5

15 NxN+

Instead of the general liquidation inaugurated with this move

122

White should have played 15 R-B1 with an enduring positional grip. Now the position is equal.

15 . . .	BxN
16 BxB	RxB
17 R-B1	P-QR4
18 P-N5	N-Q1
19 R-KB2	N-N2
20 B-B1	N-B4
21 N-B3	B-B2
22 N-Q5	

If 22 N-R4 Black replies 22... B-R4 and then plays possum with 23...R-Q1 when White cannot break through.

22 . . .	BxN
23 PxB	

DIAGRAM

23 . . .	N-Q6!

An unexpected but efficient way of enforcing the draw. If Black does nothing and relies on the strength of his knight on QB4 White may be able to organise a profitable exchange sacrifice.

24 BxN	PxB
25 QxP	QxNP
26 QxQ	RxQ
27 RxP	R-B2

Draw agreed.

After 28 R-B8+ R-B1 29 R-B6 Blacks best way to draw is 29...RxP 30 R-N2 P-N3.

(Time: 1.34 − 2.00)

GAME TWENTY-SEVEN

28th and 29th September

The duties of a world championship delegation head are many and various. On the morning of the twenty-seventh game I was entertained by City Security Chief Major Bugasto at Baguio police H.Q. Three local citizens had been arrested for demanding 15,000 dollars from Korchnoi for (unsolicited!) black magic services to help him win. The problem was that they threatened to ensure his loss if he failed to pay up. This sounded to the Baguio police more like blackmail than black magic and they decided to refer the matter to the local magistrates for a second opinion.

Before the twenty-seventh game Karpov had gone ten games without a win. Most commentators were predicting a long match and the record of thirty-five games held by Capablanca v Alekhine 1927 appeared in danger. Some critics were even claiming that Karpov had now completely run out of steam and that Korchnoi could still turn the match in his favour. I was not so optimistic. Although Korchnoi had not lost for ten games he had had three totally lost positions and he could not rely on Karpov continuing to let him of the hook.

In the twenty-seventh game Korchnoi's luck finally ran out. He obtained a good position but allowed this to deteriorate and blundered away a vital pawn in his inevitable time trouble. Korchnoi adjourned in a hopeless position and he informed me that he intended to resign on resumption. I turned up to watch the funeral rites but Korchnoi did not arrive. We were unable to contact him by telephone and so Stean drove to Korchnoi's villa to find out what had happened. He returned, brakes screeching, just in time to hand over a formal note of resignation signed by Korchnoi before Korchnoi lost on time. Apparently Korchnoi assumed I would resign on his behalf but without specific instructions I felt unable to do so. It was a little embarrassing at the time, but Korchnoi's note made it clear that there had merely been a misunderstanding and no impoliteness was intended.

Karpov now led 5-2 with 20 draws.

White: Korchnoi
Black: Karpov

English Opening

1 P-QB4   N-KB3

2 N-QB3   P-K4
3 N-B3   N-B3
4 P-KN3   B-N5
5 N-Q5   NxN

Insufficiently subtle. A better

124

alternative for Black is 5 . . . B-B4 played in the fifth Korchnoi Petrosian match game 1977.

A popular but less satisfactory alternative for Black is 5 . . . P-K5 6 N-R4 B-B4 7 B-N2 e.g. A) 7 . . . P-Q3 8 0-0 B-K3 (Ghitescu-Browne Wijk aan See 1974) and now 9 NxN+ QxN 10 BxP BxP 11 Q-R4 is good for White. B) 7 . . . 0-0 8 0-0 R-K1 9 P-Q3 PxP 10 QxP N-K4 11 Q-B2 P-B3 (Smyslov-Mecking Petropolis 1973) and now 12 NxN+ QxN 13 P-N3! is a promising sacrifice for White.

6 PxN	N-Q5
7 NxN	PxN
8 Q-B2	Q-K2
9 B-N2	

Not 9 QxP Q-K5! Now White enjoys a slight plus since his advanced QP is stronger than Black's.

9 . . .	B-B4
10 0-0	

The natural move but the forcing 10 P-QN4 may be stronger e.g. A) 10 . . . BxP 11 QxP and White has the superior pawn structure and his queen is a thorn in Black's flesh.
B) 10 . . . P-Q6 11 QxP Q-B3 12 PxB QxR and White has great compensation for the sacrificed exchange.
C) 10 . . . B-N3 11 P-QR4 P-Q6 (If 11 . . . P-QR4 12 PxP) 12 QxQP Q-B3 13 Q-K4+ K-Q1 14 R-R3 QxP+ 15 K-Q1 and White stands better in view of his central pawn mass and the superior co-ordination of his pieces.

10 . . .	0-0
11 P-K3	

A good move blocking the diagonal of Black's KB — a theme which also occurred in the twenty-fifth game.

11 . . .	B-N3
12 P-QR4	PxP?

Black mistakenly abandons control of his Q5 and brings White's position to life. Presumably his idea was to remove obstructions from the path of his KB with all possible speed, but this is strategically dubious. Better was 12 . . . P-QR4.

13 QPxP

Not a bad move but even stronger was 13 BPxP opening the KB file and envisaging a fianchetto of the QB. That would have refuted Karpov's strategy.

13 . . .	P-QR4
14 B-Q2	B-B4
15 B-QB3	P-Q3
16 Q-Q2	P-QN3
17 KR-K1	B-Q2
18 P-K4?	

White naturally wishes to advance his central pawn majority but he should have prepared the advance slowly by P-KR3 followed by K-R2 when Black can undertake nothing and must simply wait and see whether White can convert his space advantage. The disadvantage of the text is that is prematurely opens the diagonal of Black's bishop on QB4.

| 18 ... | KR-K1 |
| 19 K-R1? | |

Also weak, partly because it undefends White's KBP and partly because the idea of a pawn push with P-KB4 and P-K5 is now out of place as Karpov demonstrates with his next move.

White could have retained some advantage by 19 B-B1 intending to go to QN5 or QB4 and to consolidate his kingside with K-N2.

| 19 ... | P-QB3! |

An excellent move which blunts White's offensive and reaches clear equality. The apparent weakening of Black's QP is illusory in view of Black's bishop entrenched on QB4.

20 P-K5

Before this move Karpov had consumed one hour and twenty-five minutes while Korchnoi had only used one hour and fifteen minutes. But now Korchnoi drove his supporters berserk by thinking for forty-five minutes about — what? When we discussed the position after the game Korchnoi seemed to be suffering from the illusion that he now stood worse. But after, say, 20 P-N3 the position

is dead level. One eminent commentator (my wife!) suggested 20 B-B3 and this is also quite adequate.

20 ...	BPxP
21 BxQP	QR-Q1
22 Q-B4	Q-B1

A pretty obvious move but it seems to have baffled Korchnoi who thought for a further fifteen minutes over his reply. This left him only fifteen minutes for his next eighteen moves. The position is still drawn but Black is gaining a slight advantage due to his superior development and co-ordination.

23 Q-B3	PxP
24 BxKP	B-KN5
25 QxB	R(Q1)xB
26 B-B3	

Of course 26 BxP? fails to 26 ... RxR+ 27 RxR QxB 28 R-K8+ B-B1. Korchnoi now only had five minutes left.

| 26 ... | R(K1)-Q1! |

Quite right! Black avoids simplifications and emphasises his grip on the position.

27 K-N2	B-Q5
28 QR-B1	P-N3
29 Q-K2	Q-Q3
30 BxB	RxB

31 Q-N5??

A time trouble blunder losing a pawn. After 30 Q-B3 he could still hang on.

31 ...	**R-QN5**
32 R-K8+	**K-N2**
33 RxR	**QxR**
34 Q-K2	**Q-Q4+**
35 P-B3	

35 Q-B3 would have led to a lost rook and pawn ending.

35 ...	**RxRP**
36 R-B2	**R-Q5**
37 Q-K3	**P-QN4**
38 P-R4	**P-R4**
39 Q-K2	**P-R5**
40 Q-K3	**P-N5**
41 R-B2	**R-Q6**

The sealed move. **Korchnoi resigned** without waiting to see what it was. White's position is palpably lost.

(Times: 3.20 — 2.15)

GAME TWENTY-EIGHT

30th September and 1st October

With Karpov now only needing one more win, the vultures (who had been having a lean time since game seventeen) reassembled expectantly for the twenty-eigth game. But a defiant Korchnoi sent them away hungry.

Karpov played insipidly, as if hoping for Korchnoi to dig his own grave. But the challenger failed to oblige and until his sealed move conducted the whole of the first session in fine style. However Korchnoi jeopardised his chances of victory by sealing an inferior move. The adjourned position, although clearly favourable for Korchnoi, was extremely difficult to analyse exhaustively. We analysed furiously (without stopping for break-fast or lunch) but when we finished our analysis twenty minutes before the game was due to resume, we were still not sure whether Korchnoi had a clear win.

I could not bear to watch the first hour of the second session and stayed in my hotel room to rest. I was just preparing to set out for the playing hall when I heard familiar laughter emanating from the lift. Korchnoi had won already! Karpov had bashed out moves like a machine gun (accord-ing to Korchnoi) and contrived to lose in one hour a positon we had not been able to solve in nine hours' analysis. Korchnoi's description of how he had beaten the world champion from a possibly drawn adjourned position was: 'I simply played to get through my time trouble. When I accomplished this I relaxed, made a couple of moves and Karpov resigned.'

Karpov's conduct of the second session was amazing. If the position had been clearly lost one could have understood him invoking his old ally the clock as his last desperate hope. But the adjourned position was in fact unclear and, as it turned out, Karpov missed at least two draws in the second session. It is possible that Karpov decided on his blitz tactics on the assumption that Korchnoi had sealed one of the clearly winning moves at his disposal. Even so he should have had the presence of mind to change his tactics when confronted by an inferior sealed move.

When asked by journalists after the game if this victory signalled the start of a revival Korchnoi replied sarcastically 'Well, I won one game in a row'.

The game was widely claimed to be Korchnoi's first victory over Karpov with Black. This was not strictly true as Korchnoi had beaten Karpov twice with Black in their secret training match in 1971. It was at least his first Black win in an 'official' game.

After the game it was rumoured that Karpov's Toyota Crown official match car was involved in a minor crash on the way to his hotel at the end of the first session. Baturinsky denied that Karpov was inside but some witnesses said they saw him get out of the damaged vehicle and proceed in the police escort. Curious.

Karpov now led 5-4 with 20 draws.

White: Karpov
Black: Korchnoi

Ruy Lopez

1 P-K4	P-K4
2 N-KB3	N-QB3
3 B-N5	P-QR3
4 B-R4	N-B3
5 0-0	NxP
6 P-Q4	P-QN4
7 B-N3	P-Q4
8 PxP	B-K3
9 P-B3	N-B4
10 B-B2	B-N5

I prefer this plan to the other lines Korchnoi had adopted in this opening since it puts more pressure on White. Black may be able to play . . . BxN at some moment forcing doubled pawns which would give him real counter-chances. The drawback of Black's plan is that his QP is rather vulnerable.

11 R-K1

More dangerous for Black is 11 Q-K2 intending R-Q1 followed by P-QN4 and B-N3 or B-K4.

11 . . .	B-K2
12 QN-Q2	

An interesting try is 12 P-N4 N-K3 13 P-QR4 but that would have been rather sharp for a tired Karpov at this stage in the match.

12 . . .	Q-Q2

12 . . . P-Q5 was also playable but Korchnoi, ambitiously wanted to maintain the tension and avoid exchanges.

13 N-N3

Another possible grouping of White's pieces is 13 N-B1 R-Q1 14 N-K3 B-R4 15 N-B5 0-0 and Black has a solid position to compensate for White's strong knight on KB5.

13 . . .	N-K3

In keeping with policy indicated by Black's twelfth move.

14 P-KR3	B-R4
15 B-B5	

The pin looks annoying, but it can always be broken by . . . B-N3 or even . . . P-N3 as Korchnoi in fact later plays.

15 . . .	QN-Q1

Supporting the other knight and also planning . . . P-QB4 at an opportune moment. Black's position is a little congested but Korchnoi has at any rate succeeded in his objective of provoking a complex struggle.

16 B-K3	P-R4

A good move, preparing to force White to declare his intentions regarding the alignment of his minor pieces.

17 B-B5	P-R5
18 BxB	QxB

DIAGRAM

19 QN-Q2?

Feeble. White could not of course play 19 QxP? because of 19 . . . P-QB3. Best was 19 N(N3)-Q4

129

when White has a slight advantage.

19 . . .   P-QB3

Consolidation at last.

20 P-QN4   N-N4

Finally exploiting the pin on White's KN. It is interesting that Black's reserve knight can also gallop from Q1 via K3 to KN4.

21 Q-K2   P-N3
22 B-N4

This allows Black to gain the better ending by taking the KR file. Better was 22 B-B2 NxN+ 23 NxN N-K3 24 Q-K3 BxN 25 QxB Q-R5 when the position is equal since White's KB is restricted by the network of Black pawns on the light squares.

22 . . .   BxB
23 PxB   QN-K3
24 Q-K3   P-R4
25 NxN   QxN
26 QxQ   NxQ
27 PxP   RxP

Korchnoi had played well so far and managed to obtain a slightly better positon. This was nothing new. What was new was that he now managed to continue to play well in the crucial final hour of the first session despite being in time trouble.

28 N-B1   R-R5
29 QR-Q1   K-K2

30 P-B3   N-K3
31 N-K3   R-Q1

Black finally abandons any intention of castling.

32 N-N4   N-N2
33 N-K3   N-K3
34 N-N4   N-N2
35 N-K3   N-B4

Although short of time (he had about five minutes left) Korchnoi spurns repetition. He has a long-term advantage based on the superior compactness of Black's queenside pawns and Whites dead point at K5, which looks aggressive but turns out to be a liability.

36 N-B2?

Why not 36 N-N4? The text (and 36 NxN+ which would also be a mistake) allows Black's rook to reach an ideal square on his QB5.

36 . . .   R-QB5
37 R-Q3   P-Q5!!

A very deep move played in high time trouble. Korchnoi was twitching and fidgeting in his seat before playing this move and I thought he had overlooked White's next move. But, although Korchnoi had less than a minute left, everything was under control.

38 P-N4   N-N2
39 NxP   N-K3!

Now everything becomes clear. Black will obtain a vastly superior ending in which White is burdened with weak points.

40 KR-Q1   NxN
41 PxN   RxNP
42 K-B2

DIAGRAM

42 . . .   P-QB4?

The sealed move which is a

mistake although Korchnoi took thirty-eight minutes over it. Stronger was either 42 . . . K-K3 or 42 . . . R-N7+ 43 R(Q1)-Q2 RxR+ 44 RxR P-N5 when White has no counterchances as Black's king has a free path to K3 and Q4.

43 P-Q5

Probably not best. Our analysis also considered the following possibilities:

A) 43 PxP RxR 44 RxR R-N7+ and 45 . . . RxRP winning.
B1) 43 K-K3 R(Q1)xP? 44 RxR PxR+ 45 RxP R-N7 46 K-K4 P-R6 (If 46 . . . RxP 47 R-N4 is equal) 47 R-Q5 P-N5 48 R-N5 K-Q2 49 K-Q5 RxP 50 R-N7+ K-Q1 51 RxNP R-R8 52 R-Q4 P-R7 53 R-Q2 P-N4 (otherwise 54 P-B4 draws) 54 P-K6 (54 K-K4+ K-K2 55 K-B5 also draws) K-K2 55 PxP KxP 56 K-Q6 with a draw.
B2) 43 K-K3 P-B5! and now Black has winning chances though we had not sorted out all the possibilities before resumption. If 44 R-B3 R-N7 wins for Black. The position is not so clear after 44 R(Q3)-Q2 but Black still has chances after 46 . . . P-R6 planning 47 . . . R-N7.

| 43 . . . | R-N7+ |
| 44 K-N3 | |

The king would be exposed on K3 and anyway Black wants that square for his rook.

| 44 . . . | RxRP? |

Korchnoi forgot our analysis! The correct move was 44 . . . P-N4! dislocating White's kingside pawns and threatening 45 . . . R-KR1 with a mating net. One variation is 44 . . . P-N4 45 P-K6 PxP 46 R-K3 R-Q3 and Black should win.

| 45 R-K3 | P-N5 |
| 46 P-K6 | |

White should now draw and he is even threatening to win by 47 P-Q6+.

| 46 . . . | R-R6 |
| 47 R-K2? | |

Also bad was 47 P-Q6+ RxP 48 RxR(Q6) RxR and Black wins but White could have drawn by 47 RxR! PxR 48 PxP+ KxP 49 K-B4 and Black will not be able to hold his split queenside pawns.

47 . . .	PxP
48 RxP+	K-B2
49 R(Q1)-K1	

Karpov, still playing at full speed, misses his last chance which was 49 P-N5 threatening a series of checks starting with 50 R-B6+. It is possible White could then still draw.

49 . . .	R-Q2
50 R-N6	R-Q6
51 R(K1)-K6	R(Q6)xP
52 RxKNP	P-R6
53 R(N6)-B6+	K-K2
54 R(B6)-K6+	K-B1
55 R-B6+	K-K2
56 R(N6)-K6+	K-Q1
57 R-QR6	R-QN2
58 R-B8+	K-B2

59 R-B7+	R-Q2
60 R-B5	P-N6
61 RxP(B5)+	K-N1

DIAGRAM

White has run out of checks and he cannot prevent one of Black's advanced pawns queening. **Karpov therefore resigned.**
(Approximate times: 2.45 — 3.35. The deputy chief arbiter forgot to record the exact times!)

GAME TWENTY-NINE

7th and 8th October

Korchnoi's win in game twenty-eight showed that he was not prepared to surrender the match without a fight. But the sword of Damocles remained suspended precariously over his head. However many games the match might continue he knew that in every remaining game one blunder (and he had made all too many so far) could bring the match to an abrupt end.

The tension increased when the twenty-ninth game was twice postponed. On the Tuesday that the game was originally due to be played an explosion in the generator plunged the Playing Hall into darkness only one hour before the game was due to start. The generator was known to be a sickly specimen and so foul play was not suspected. The frantic application of smelling salts, spanners and glue resuscitated the generator in time for play to start of the Thursday.

But in the meantime there had been another casualty. Korchnoi had spent his free day on the beach. Alas he stayed too long. He returned badly sunburnt and had to postpone the game from Thursday to Saturday. On Saturday he had still not recovered from his sunburn and had caught a cold as well. But he was not entitled to any more postponements and so he had to play.

When Korchnoi arrived for the postponed twenty-ninth game someone remarked that he looked like a fluorescent carrot. But his play did not appear to be affected and after nurturing a slight positional advantage he adjourned with a small plus. This should not have been enough to win but once again Karpov tried to blitz him in time trouble and it was the champion who produced the decisive errors. Korchnoi's conduct of the game was well-nigh flawless but the same cannot be said of Karpov. After the game Korchnoi attributed his victory to Karpov's mistakes but added that he was proud of his own fighting spirit. He said to Edmondson 'Fischer respects me because of this. Everyone else he can intimidate with his own fighting spirit, but not me.'

Karpov's defeat must have been all the more galling because Vasyukov had arrived to help him accompanied by the USSR Chess Federation President, Sebastianov, an ex-cosmonaut. Presumably Sebastianov had arrived for the supposedly imminent closing ceremony!

Karpov now led 5-4, with 20 draws.

White: Korchnoi
Black: Karpov

English Opening

1 P-QB4	N-KB3
2 N-QB3	P-K3
3 P-K4	P-B4
4 P-K5	N-N1
5 P-Q4	

Korchnoi has adopted a line of the English Opening favoured by Nimzowitsch, Keene and others, but he now rejects the pawn sacrifice 5 N-B3 N-QB3 6 P-Q4 PxP 7 NxP NxP with which I beat Karpov's late trainer Furman at Bad Lauterberg last year. The move Korchnoi adopts has been dismissed by theory as too drawish but the Korchnoi camp had worked out some improvements.

5 ...	PxP
6 QxP	N-QB3
7 Q-K4	P-Q3
8 N-B3	PxP
9 NxP	N-B3

Korchnoi's choice of opening has been a success as Karpov had now used almost an hour against Korchnoi's four minutes.

Instead of the text which weakens Black's pawn structure theory regards 9 . . . B-Q2 as best.

10 NxN	Q-N3
11 Q-B3	PxN
12 B-K2	

12 P-KN3 planning B-N2 to hinder . . . P-QB4 may be an improvement.

12 ...	B-N2
13 0-0	P-B4
14 Q-R3	B-K2

DIAGRAM

15 B-B3

I had expected Korchnoi to play 15 P-QN3 and followed by B-N2 and B-Q3 aiming his bishops at Black's king.

Instead Korchnoi adopts a highly positional plan which aims to leave Black with a bad bishop hemmed in by the pawn on Black's QB4.

15 ...	0-0
16 P-QN3	KR-Q1
17 B-K3	B-B3
18 N-R4	Q-B2
19 BxB	QxB
20 QR-Q1	QR-B1
21 Q-N3	B-Q3
22 Q-R4	B-K2
23 P-B3	K-B1
24 Q-B2	RxR
25 RxR	Q-B2
26 Q-N3	

Exchanging queens does not indicate any pacific intentions on Korchnoi's part. It is consistent with Korchnoi's policy of accentuating the limitations of Black's KB.

26 ...	QxQ
27 PxQ	P-KR4
28 K-B2	K-K1
29 K-K2	P-N3
30 N-B3	P-R3
31 N-R4	R-B3
32 R-KR1	B-Q3

33 B-B2	N-Q2
34 P-KN4	

A surprising but fully justified decision. White's doubled pawns tie Black down and White's rook becomes active.

34 ...	PxP
35 R-R8+	K-K2
36 PxP	P-N4
37 B-K3	P-B3
38 N-B3	K-B2
39 R-R7+	K-K1
40 N-K4	B-K2

41 R-R6

The sealed move over which Korchnoi took thirty-six minutes and forty-five seconds. He had already lost his early lead on the clock and he now left himself with only twenty-seven minutes to reach move 56.

It was painful to watch his indecision on the stage. He thought for fifteen minutes, got up and hid in a corner of the stage (to circumvent prying eyes, I imagine). He then wrote down a sealed move, came back and sat slumped over the board. After a further ten minutes he crossed out his move and repeated the performance, finally sealing the text.

Golombek won four bottles of whisky by correctly guessing the sealed move but in fact it is not best! After 41 B-Q2, aiming to transfer the bishop to QB3 as quickly as possible Black is subjected to intolerable pressure.

41 ...	K-B2

We spent a long time analysing 41 . . . P-R4 which weakens Black's position but is his only chance for active couterplay. We decided it was too risky for Black e.g. 42 R-R8+ N-B1 43 B-Q2 R-R3 44 B-B3 K-B2 45 R-R6 and now:
A) 45 . . . K-N2 46 RxP BxR 47 BxB+ K-N3 48 NxBP and White should win.
B) 45 . . . N-Q2 46 R-R7+ K-K1 (This line shows how Black is squeezed when White's bishop reaches QB3) 47 P-R4 P-B4 48 PxP PxP 49 N-N3 P-B5 50 N-B5 B-B3 51 BxRP and White trickily wins a pawn since Black dare not capture the bishop in view of 52 N-Q6+.

42 R-R7+	K-B1
43 R-R8+	K-B2
44 B-Q2	

The direct method was 44 R-R8 when I had analysed the line 44 . . . N-K4 45 R-R7 K-K1 46 N-B2 P-B4 47 B-Q2 B-B3! (taking White's KNP leaves Black very passive) 48 B-R5 NxP 49 NxN PxN 50 B-B7 and Black is paralysed. One winning idea is K-K3 followed by K-K4 and B-K5. However 48 . . . N-Q2 planning 49 . . . B-Q5 is a much tougher defence to crack.

Instead of adopting the direct approach Korchnoi decides to tack around. Since he only had twenty minutes to reach move 56 I wondered if he was using his time trouble as a kind of provocation to lure Karpov to play incautiously.

| 44 ... | N-B1 |
| 45 R-R1 | |

More tacking.

| 45 ... | K-N3 |
| 46 R-Q1 | P-B4? |

Too risky since it exposes the central White squares. Korchnoi only had ten minutes now but Karpov had been successfully provoked.

47 N-B2	B-Q3
48 B-B3	N-Q2
49 PxP+	PxP
50 P-KN4!	

Exchanges help White since both his minor pieces are superior to their opposite numbers and Black's pawns are exposed.

| 50 ... | N-N3 |

Not 50 ... P-B5 51 N-K4!

51 K-B3	B-K2
52 B-R5	R-B3
53 K-N2	PxP
54 NxP	R-K3
55 K-B3	B-B3
56 NxB	

On his last move before the second time control Korchnoi makes the right decision. Earlier Black's bishop had been a problem piece but now it was threatening to entrench itself on Q5. After the exchange White's bishop is much stronger than Black's knight.

56 ...	RxN+
57 K-N4	N-B1
58 B-Q8	R-B5+
59 K-N3	R-B4
60 P-R4	

White plans P-R5 and B-N6. If White wins a pawn by 60 R-Q7

R-B2 61 RxR KxR 62 BxP Black can draw by rushing his king to QB3. Black should also be able to draw after 60 R-Q5 since after the rook swap White's RP if of the wrong colour for his bishop.

| 60 ... | K-B2 |

Better was 60 ... R-K4.

| 61 R-Q3 | R-K4 |
| 62 K-N4 | K-N3 |

So Black has lost a tempo.

| 63 P-R5 | R-K5+ |
| 64 K-B3 | |

| 64 ... | R-B5+? |

The losing move. 64 ... K-B4 was probably still good enough to draw e.g. 65 BxP N-R2 activating the Black knight or 65 R-Q5+ R-K4 and Black gives up his KNP and rushes his king to QB3. Korchnoi was again in terrible time trouble (for the second time in the session) and Karpov was provoked into another misguided attempt to blitz him.

65 K-K3	R-R5
66 R-Q5	R-R6+
67 K-Q2	RxP
68 RxP	R-N1
69 R-B6+	K-B4
70 RxP	P-N5
71 R-B6+	K-K5
72 B-B7	R-N7+

73 K-B3	R-N2	76 B-N3	R-N8
74 B-R2	R-KR2	77 R-B4+	K-K6
75 B-N8		78 R-B8	N-K2
		79 P-R6	

Both players continued to play at lightning speed even though the time control had been reached at move 72. Karpov now paused for a while to survey the tatters of his position.

75 . . .	R-QN2

If 79 . . . N-B3 80 P-R7 NxP 81 B-B2+ wins the knight. Karpov therefore **resigned** by signing the score sheet and hurrying from the stage.

(Times: 4.54—4.15)

GAME THIRTY

Korchnoi's win in game twenty-eight had indicated that the challenger was not prepared simply to lie down and die. His win in the twenty-ninth game did much more. For the first time since Karpov achieved a three game lead by winning the seventeenth game, the whole result of the match really seemed in doubt.

There were suggestions that Karpov had cracked in games twenty-eight and twenty-nine but I think this is an oversimplification. His play had in fact been patchy for some time, but then so had Korchnoi's. What marked the twenty-eighth and twenty-ninth games was that Korchnoi seemed to have got his second wind and was not leaving Karpov's mistakes unpunished. If Korchnoi could keep it up Karpov needed to raise his own level of play to finish the match off.

The public had been rather spoilt by the recent rich diet of three decisive games. In game thirty they were served much humbler fare. The advantage fluctuated slightly but the game always seemed to be heading for the draw which was finally agreed after forty-two moves. Karpov must have been relieved to stop the rot, but Korchnoi could also be well satisfied with a comfortable draw with Black.

With the completion of game thirty the match reached another milestone. It equalled the number of games of the 1935 encounter between Alekhine and Euwe. In both matches the score stood at 15½—14½ but there was the important difference that this was the final score in 1935.

One more landmark beckoned — the thirty-five games of the 1927 Capablanca—Alekhine match. It is interesting that the present match had already lasted longer in terms of days than the 1927 encounter. Needing so few rest days maybe the 1927 contestants really were made of sterner stuff!

Karpov now led 5-4 with 21 draws.

White: Karpov
Black: Korchnoi

English Opening

1 P-QB4	N-KB3
2 N-QB3	P-Q4

The game now transposes into a kind of Grunfeld Defence on which Korchnoi is a leading expert.

The first game in which the Grunfeld Defence proper was played in international chess was Alekhine-Grunfeld Vienna 1922. I believe that is the game which Alekhine resigned by hurling his king across the room!

3 PxP	NxP
4 P-KN3	P-KN3
5 B-N2	NxN
6 NPxN	B-N2
7 N-B3	0-0
8 0-0	P-QB4
9 R-N1	N-B3
10 Q-R4	N-R4
11 P-Q3	P-N3
12 Q-R4	B-N2
13 B-R6	BxB
14 QxB	BxN
15 BxB	R-B1
16 B-N2	Q-Q2
17 QR-K1	P-QN4

18 R-N1

An indecisive move since the rook has only just moved to K1. After the game 18 P-KB4 was widely recommended but Korchnoi's intended 18 . . . Q-Q3 and if 19 P-B5, Q-K4 is a perfectly adequate response.

18 . . .	R-N1
19 Q-K3	Q-Q3
20 KR-Q1	P-QR3

After White's indecision, Black enjoys a slight advantage which he could have retained by playing 20 . . . R-N3 now or on the next move.

21 R-Q2	KR-B1
22 R(Q2)-N2	N-B3
23 Q-Q2	N-K4

23 . . . R-N3 was still the right move. Now the initiative passes back to White but it is nothing serious.

24 Q-B4	N-Q2
25 QxQ	PxQ
26 B-R3	R-Q1
27 P-R4	PxP
28 BxN	RxR
29 RxR	RxB
30 R-R2	K-B1
31 RxP	R-R2
32 K-B1	K-K2
33 K-K1	K-Q2
34 K-Q2	P-KR4

Here Korchnoi offered a draw through the Arbiter. Karpov declined by playing another move without comment. This may seem impolite but it wasn't. It is a perfectly legitimate and commonly adopted means of declining a draw.

35 K-B2	R-R1
36 R-KB4	K-K3
37 P-R4	R-QN1
38 R-K4+	K-Q2
39 R-R4	R-QR1
40 R-KB4	K-K3
41 R-B4	R-R2
42 R-K4+	

The sealed move which strictly forms part of the game even though it was never played on the board. One and a half hours before play was due to be resumed I accepted on behalf of Korchnoi Karpov's offer of a **draw** which was relayed through the acting chief arbiter Filip.

(Times:)

GAME THIRTY-ONE

12th and 13th October

Korchnoi believes that thirteen is his lucky number. This may seem perverse since he lost disastrously in the thirteenth game of the present match as he had done in the thirteenth game of the Candidates' final against Spassky. But it was on Friday the thirteenth in game 31 (the reverse of 13!?!) that he stunned the chess world by equalising the score at 5-5.

The game started quietly. Korchnoi built up a slight advantage by adopting an unusual plan in a well-known variation. He wisely refrained from forcing the issue until after the time control and Karpov made no attempt to compel him to do so. After the time control (but still in the first session) Korchnoi finally broke the position open and Karpov should probably then have adjourned to give himself time to work out how to defend. But he continued playing until move 47, by which time his position had become critical. After the game Tal claimed the adjourned position was already lost for Karpov, but our adjournment analysis had unearthed resources for Karpov against which we were unable to find a clear win. As it was Karpov failed to find the best defence and Korchnoi finished him off in ruthless style. Although the earlier stages of the game were rather tedious the ending should find its way into all the text books as a classic demonstration of the importance of active pieces and mobile pawns in rook and pawn endings.

Korchnoi's victory in this game heralded the most spectacular comeback ever witnessed in a world championship match. Steinitz had recovered from 4-1 down against Zukertort in 1886 and Euwe was twice three games down before beating Alekhine in 1935. What marked out Korchnoi's achievement was that it was performed while the sword of Damocles was poised over his head ready to end the whole match if he made a single mistake.

After the game Korchnoi declared that the chances in the match were now equal and that the result was a lottery. To observers, however, it appeared to be a lottery in which Korchnoi held most of the tickets.

The score was now 5-5 with 21 draws.

White: Korchnoi	1 P-QB4	P-K3
Black: Karpov	2 N-QB3	P-Q4
	3 P-Q4	N-KB3
Queen's Gambit Declined	4 PxP	

Karpov has varied from the English Opening with which he failed to achieve equality in the twenty-ninth game. For the first time in the match Korchnoi now opts for a straight exchange variation of the Queen's Gambit.

4 . . .	PxP
5 B-N5	B-K2
6 P-K3	0-0
7 B-Q3	QN-Q2
8 N-B3	R-K1
9 Q-B2	P-B3
10 0-0	N-B1
11 BxN	BxB
12 P-QN4	B-N5
13 N-Q2	R-B1

It seems more sensible for Black to preserve his QB by e.g. 13 . . . B-R4.

14 B-B5	BxB
15 QxB	Q-Q2

So far we have been following the game Miagmasuren-Reshevsky Sousse 1967 in which Black played 15 . . . P-KN3. Having played the opening moves quickly, Karpov stopped for a long think before offering the exchange of queens. In my opinion he made the wrong decision since the simplification gives White a freer hand and reduces Black's chances of kingside play.

Before the match the Korchnoi camp considered that Karpov was an expert in simplified positions but not so good in complications. The present game in combination with Karpov's previous two losses suggests that he is also ill at ease in complex positions without queens.

16 QxQ	NxQ
17 P-QR4	B-K2
18 KR-N1	N-B3

19 P-R5

A very interesting plan. By sealing the queenside Korchnoi makes Black's QNP a permanent liability and prepares a long-term central break with P-K4. The idea is that after vast exchanges on the king's file Black's QNP will be very vulnerable to a White knight on QB5. The only drawback is the lack of mobility in White's queenside infantry.

19 . . .	P-QR3
20 N-R4	B-B1
21 N-B5	R-K2
22 K-B1	N-K1
23 K-K2	N-Q3
24 K-Q3	QR-K1
25 R-K1	P-KN3

Hereabouts the Russians (Tal, Vasiukov, Zaitsev etc.) were claiming an advantage for Black. Euwe was very scathing about this: 'They are entitled to their opinion but I know White is better!' He obviously had in mind his win against Alekhine from Zurich 1934 in which he employed a similar strategy, but with queens on the board. He took great delight in making his point by repeatedly slaughtering Baturinsky from this position in the press room.

26 R-K2	P-B3

Karpov is pussyfooting about. At some stage he should have taken his life in his hands and played 26 . . . P-KB4, even though it weakens his K4 square. Korchnoi said that one of Karpov's main weaknesses was in allowing himself to be taken by the throat before he truly started to fight.

27 QR-K1	B-R3
28 N(2)-N3	B-B1
29 N-Q2	B-R3
30 P-R3	K-B2
31 P-N4	B-B1
32 P-B3	R-Q1
33 N(2)-N3	N-N4
34 R-KB1	B-R3
35 P-B4	

White would like to play P-K4 but then Black could settle his bishop on KB5.

35 . . .	B-B1
36 N-Q2	N-Q3
37 R(1)-K1	P-R3
38 R-KB1	R-N1
39 R-QR1	R(1)-K1
40 R(1)-K1	R-N1
41 P-K4	

At last. Korchnoi had been in time trouble and so delayed this expected advance until after the time control.

41 . . .	PxP
42 N(2)xP	N-N4

Setting a trap. 43 P-B5 now looks very promising but Black can play 43 . . . PxP 44 PxP R-Q1 45 N-K6 RxP+! 46 NxR R-Q2 with enormous counterplay.

43 N-B3	RxR
44 RxR	BxN
45 NPxB	R-Q1
46 NxN	RPxN

47 P-B5

Korchnoi's original idea was 47 R-QR2 but he changed his mind. Up to now Karpov had been moving with his usual speed and had taken about one hour less than Korchnoi. He now decided to adjourn and took twenty minutes on his sealed move. Since the time control he had taken two crucial decisions in exchanging both pairs of minor pieces. Both of these decisions may have been correct (I am not certain myself) but since Karpov had time in hand surely it would have been more prudent to adjourn and consider them at leisure.

A complex position. Superficially it might appear that White's weak pawns on QR5 and Q4 give Black some advantage. In reality it is White who has the chances since his powerful horns on QB5 and KB5 cramp Black and represent dangerous potential passed pawns. White's winning plans (all involving pawn sacrifices) are based on the annexation of the Black pawns on Black's QB3 and KB3. One idea is P-QR6 followed by K-B3-N4-R5-N6 and another is R-K6 followed by P-R6.

47 . . .	PxP
48 PxP	R-KN1

If 48 . . . R-K1 white plays 49 R-QR2 not 49 P-Q5 R-Q1 50 P-Q6 R-K1 which is a draw.

49 K-B3

Less obvious than 49 R-QR2 with the idea of P-R6, which is also better for White but clearer to defend.

49 . . .	R-K1?

Better was 49 . . . R-N8 when Korchnoi intended to play the risky line 50 P-R6 PxP 51 R-K6 P-QR4 52 RxQBP R-N6+ 53 K-Q2 when both sides get connected passed pawns. White's chances are better but there is no clear cut win. Winning White's irrelevant KRP by 49 . . . R-N6+ would be suicidal after 50 K-N4 RxP 51 P-R6 PxP 52 K-R5 followed by 53 K-N6 etc. In this ending it is the quality of pawns which counts more than their quantity.

50 R-Q2	R-K5

We had not considered this. Stronger is 50 . . . R-K8 51 P-Q5 R-B8+ and if 52 R-B2 R-QR8! Better for White is 52 K-N2 RxP 53 PxP when White still has some chances. The text prevents P-Q5 but does not impede P-R6.

51 K-N4	K-K1

52 P-R6	PxP
53 K-R5	K-Q2
54 K-N6	

Now Black can do nothing to prevent the crushing P-Q5, clearing the path for White's QBP.

54 . . .	P-N5
55 P-Q5	PxP
56 RxP+	K-B1
57 R-Q3	

Aiming to seize the KN file.

57 . . .	P-QR4
58 R-KN3	P-N6
59 K-B6	

Not at once 59 RxP??, R-N5+ and Black wins.

59 . . .	K-N1
60 RxP+	

The ending has now turned into a rout. White picks up Black's pawns at his leisure.

60 . . .	K-R2
61 R-N7+	K-R3
62 R-N6+	K-R2
63 K-N5	P-R5
64 RxP	R-KB5
65 RxP	P-R6
66 R-R6+	K-N1
67 RxP	RxP
68 R-KN3	R-B3
69 R-N8+	K-B2
70 R-N7+	K-B1
71 R-KR7	resigns

GAME THIRTY-TWO

After the buffeting he had been receiving recently nobody was surprised when Karpov decided to postpone the thirty-second game. He spent his time relaxing in Manila while Korchnoi stayed in Baguio entertaining journalists by standing on his head and performing other yoga exercises.

The Russians pulled out all the stops for what everyone sensed would be the final game. On the morning of the game they called a meeting of the jury and demanded that the Ananda Margas should be removed from Korchnoi's *private* villa. Since they were on bail pending the result of their appeal this demand contradicted their rights under the Philippino constitution. But the jury (which had unfortunately lost the moderating influence of Euwe, who had just left Baguio) did not seem to care. When it became clear that the vote was going to go 5-2 against me I reluctantly gave way and agreed to do my best to remove the Ananda Margas from Korchnoi's villa. Since nothing had changed since the Russians had accepted the compromise whereby the Ananda Margas were to be confined to Korchnoi's villa, why did they suddenly bring the matter up again at this stage? Could the score in the match possibly have had anything to do with it?

When the thirty-second game started who should be sitting in the fourth row of the audience but our old friend Dr. Zukhar? This clear breach of the agreement that he should sit at the back of the hall at least relieved me from the undertaking which I had given, under duress, regarding the Ananda Margas.

After all the efforts which had been made to ensure he won it would have been ungrateful of Karpov not to produce his best form in the final game. He duly obliged but Korchnoi was unrecognisable as the lion who had roared in the four previous games. Karpov broke through the centre in classic style and the final stages of the game witnessed an anti-climatic mopping up operation. Korchnoi adjourned but his position was obviously hopeless and his heroic challenge ended with a whimper when he resigned without resumption. As a final gesture of defiance he refused to sign the score sheet in protest against the pressure to which he had been subjected in the final game.

So after three months and thirty-two games the match was over at last.
Final score: Karpov 6, Korchnoi 5, with 21 draws.

White: Karpov
Black: Korchnoi

Pirc Defence

1 P-K4	P-Q3
2 P-Q4	N-KB3
3 N-QB3	P-KN3
4 N-B3	B-N2
5 B-K2	0-0
6 0-0	P-B4

Korchnoi varies from the standard 6 . . . B-N5 which he played in the eighteenth game. The text leads to a position more commonly reached by the move order 1 P-Q4 P-QB4 2 P-Q5 N-KB3 3 N-QB3 P-Q3 4 P-K4 P-KN3 5 N-B3 B-N2 6 0-0 0-0 — an unusual and rather dubious variation championed by the chief arbiter of the present match, Lothar Schmid. This variation produces an uncompromising struggle, which is what Korchnoi wanted. In retrospect it might have been more circumspect to play a quieter defence with Black with a view to drawing this game and winning with White in game thirty-three. But after Karpov's recent collapse who can blame Korchnoi for trying to finish the match in the present game?

7 P-Q5	N-R3
8 B-KB4	N-B2
9 P-QR4	P-N3
10 R-K1	B-N2
11 B-B4	N-R4?
12 B-KN5	N-B3

An admission that his last move was a mistake. If 12 . . . P-KR3 13 B-R4 P-KN4 14 N-Q2! is better for White.

13 Q-Q3	P-QR3
14 QR-Q1	R-N1
15 P-R3	N-Q2

16 Q-K3	B-QR1
17 B-R6	P-QN4

Black has obtained his strategic objective of expanding on the queenside but it does not achieve very much. The play now revolves round White's attempt to achieve his strategic objective — the advance P-K5. If he can play this move in favourable circumstances his space advantage will guarantee him the better game.

18 BxB	KxB
19 B-B1	N-B3
20 PxP	PxP
21 N-K2	B-N2
22 N-N3	QR-R1
23 P-B3	R-R5
24 B-Q3	Q-R1

Black is trying to prevent P-K5 by piling up on White's QP so that the advance of the KP will leave the QP too exposed. But White gets in P-K5 anyway through a tactical trick. Better, therefore, was 24 . . . K-R1 holding up the advance.

25 P-K5!	PxP

If Black had played 24 . . . K-R1 he could now have refuted White's central thrust by 25 . . . QNxP but this now loses to 26 PxN *check*. It seams that Black could have played 25 . . . KNxP but then comes the crushing 26 N-R5+!! mating e.g. 26 . . . K-N1 27 Q-R6 or 26 . . . PxN 27 Q-N5+ K-R1 28 Q-R6 P-B4 29 N-N5. Korchnoi denies Karpov the satisfaction of finishing the match off in this elegant manner but he is now strategically lost anyway.

| 26 QxKP | NxP |
| 27 BxQNP | R-R2 |

27 . . . R-R4 trying to bolster up the weakling QBP may be an improvement. But White should still win by combining threats against the Black king with pressure on the Black QBP

28 N-R4

Threatening (either) N-B5+.

28 . . .	B-B1
29 B-K2	B-K3
30 P-QB4	N-N5
31 QxBP	

White is now a pawn up with the better position. Normally Korchnoi would have resigned about now but in the circumstances he chooses to fight on to the bitter end. The final few moves represent a tragic climax to Korchnoi's bid for the world championship. Fortunately he was too short of time to consider the pathos of the situation.

31 . . .	Q-N1
32 B-B1	R-B1
33 Q-KN5	K-R1
34 R-Q2	N-B3
35 Q-R6	R-N1
36 N-KB3	Q-KB1
37 Q-K3	K-N2
38 N-N5	B-Q2
39 P-N4	Q-R1
40 P-N5	N-R4
41 P-N6	R-N2

The sealed move. **Korchnoi resigned** without resuming.

CONCLUSION

Anatoly Karpov won the world chess championship in 1975 without playing a game, but it took him 32 gruelling games to retain his title in 1978. Here is a summary of how he did it.

	Karpov	Korchnoi	Opening	Number of moves
1	½	½	Queen's Gambit	18
2	½	½	RuyLopez	29
3	½	½	Nimzo-Indian Defence	30
4	½	½	Ruy Lopez	19
5	½	½	Nimzo-Indian Defence	124
6	½	½	English Opening	23
7	½	½	Nimzo-Indian Defence	42
8	1	0	Ruy Lopez	28
9	½	½	Queen's Gambit	41
10	½	½	Ruy Lopez	44
11	0	1	Sicilian Defence	51
12	½	½	Ruy Lopez	44
13	1	0	Queen's Gambit	61
14	1	0	Ruy Lopez	50
15	½	½	Catalan Opening	25
16	½	½	French Defence	42
17	1	0	Nimzo-Indian Defence	39
18	½	½	Pirc Defence	64
19	½	½	Catalan Opening	39
20	½	½	Caro Kann Defence	63
21	0	1	Queen's Gambit	60
22	½	½	French Defence	64
23	½	½	Queen's Gambit	41
24	½	½	Ruy Lopez	45
25	½	½	English Opening	80
26	½	½	English Opening	27
27	1	0	English Opening	41
28	0	1	Ruy Lopez	61
29	0	1	English Opening	79
30	½	½	English Opening	42
31	0	1	Queen's Gambit	71
32	1	0	Pirc Defence	41

Final score: Karpov 6 wins, Korchnoi 5 wins, 21 draws.

The match divides naturally into four phases. During the first (Games 1-12) Korchnoi clearly had the better of the play but he was only able to convert one of his advantageous positions into a win. With the score standing at 1-1 with 10 draws Karpov had ceased to be firm favourite and the result of the match appeared to be completely open. But the second phase (Games 13-17) changed all that. Karpov won three more games without reply and the question in most people's minds became not who would win but how long Korchnoi could make the match last. The third phase (Games 18-26) was in many ways the reverse of the first. Now it was Karpov who established good positions only to throw them away. Korchnoi managed to pull back one game during this phase but this still left him trailing 4-3.

The fourth phase (Games 27-32) produced the final shoot-out. Karpov won game 27 to go 5-2 up but then appeared to run out of ammunition. Korchnoi scored 3½ points from the next four games to level the score at 5-5. It looked as though a miracle was about to occur but it was not to be. Karpov won the thirty-second game and retained his title by the narrowest possible margin, 6-5.

So Karpov remains world chess champion for at least another three years. It is curious that his chess-playing reputation should actually have suffered as a result of a match he won, but such undoubtedly is the case. During the three years before the match he bestrode the chess world like a colossus and acquired a reputation for near-invincibility. But Korchnoi changed all that by winning five games and letting Karpov off the hook in several more. During his three years in clover Karpov was renowned for doing nothing in particular but doing it very well. In this match he continued to do little but Korchnoi was able to show that much of what he did was wrong. This was partly due to Karpov's handling of the clock. He had obviously decided this was Korchnoi's Achilles' heel and he played on this weakness constantly. He played fast (superficially?) to induce Korchnoi to get into time trouble and played double-edged (rash?) moves when Korchnoi was in time trouble. In the end this unaesthetic tactic worked but it came perilously close to costing Karpov the match. It would have been a better match, and probably Karpov would have obtained a better result, if Karpov had used his full time allowance and concentrated on trying to find the best moves. For all these criticisms, one cannot take away from Karpov the fact that he won the match and so established himself as the most effective player in the world today.

Korchnoi played better than Karpov — but he also played worse. His play was generally on a higher creative plane than Karpov's. But too often his play descended briefly but decisively to the depths. Nearly always these lapses were caused by his perennial enemy, the clock. It was easy enough to spot the disease but it proved impossible to find a cure. Korchnoi failed to win the world title but he took the champion the full distance and his play at its best was worthy of any world champion. He deserves to be ranked alongside Tarrasch Rubinstein and Keres as one of the greatest players never to win the world championship.

The match was marred by some spectacular blunders which may give a misleading impression of the overall quality of the play. Blunders have occurred in all previous world championship matches, but the rose-tinted contact lenses through which those matches are now viewed have not yet been donned by the commentators on the present match. Let there be no doubt that the general quality of the play was high. In the three years before the match the contestants had not played one another but in their separate spheres of combat each had established himself as a well-nigh irresistible force. Logic required that they could not both be immovable objects and so, after sparks had flown in all directions and both players had tottered, it was Korchnoi who finally fell. But before he did the chess world had been entertained and instructed by varied and original opening play, fiercely contested middle games and skilfully conducted endings. The games will be profitably studied for many years to come.

This was not the first world championship to be conducted against a backcloth of hate but I think it was the worst. Previous matches have been soured by personal antipathy (e.g. Lasker v Tarrasch 1908 and Capablanca v Alekhine 1927) or ideological differences (e.g. Spassky v Fischer 1972). The present match was afflicted by both these problems to a greater degree than ever before and the situation was exacerbated by the fact that the cross-currents of controversy swept up not only the players themselves but also members of their delegations, the organisers and members of the jury. The bones of contention which arose in this hostile atmosphere included not only matters of genuine importance but also trivia which could have easily been buried if only the ground had been less frosty.

How this fractious atmosphere affected Karpov I find hard to judge. He maintained an unruffled exterior and may indeed have been more immune to disturbance than Korchnoi but I am sure he cannot have been totally unaffected. I know only too well how the atmosphere affected Korchnoi. Among the many disrupting factors I will single out the Zukhar Dispute. There is no doubt in my mind that this contributed substantially to Korchnoi's disastrous performance in games 13-17. Whether or not Korchnoi's fears were justified, chess matches should not be influenced by factors such as this.

The spectre of Bobby Fischer haunted the whole match. There were many who claimed that Fischer would have easily beaten either of the jerks who were presumptuously fighting for his title. The situation was similar to the match between Steinitz and Anderssen in 1866 held between the best two players in the world except the retired Paul Morphy. I regard the Fischer question as basically irrelevant. I know he was a superb player in 1972 and I would be very interested to know whether, weighed down by the accumulation of six years' mildew, he can play to anywhere near the some standard now. If so, let him come out of retirement and prove it (Morphy never did). If not, let the disputation of chess honours be left to those who are prepared to play. Fischer denied the chess world the spectacle of a world championship match in 1975. In 1978, despite all the problems, Karpov and Korchnoi laid on a thirty-two game banquet for the hungry chess world. We must all be grateful to them for this magnificent feast.

Part III
_____ Appendix _____
DOCUMENTS
RELATING TO THE
MATCH

To
L. I. Brezhnev
General Secretary of the Communist Party
President of the Supreme Soviet of the USSR
Marshall of the USSR

V. L. Korchnoi
Int. Chess Grandmaster
Challenger for the World
Chess Championship
Resident in Switzerland

Open Letter

Dear Mr. Brezhnev,

As a professional chess grandmaster, recently a citizen of the USSR, now resident in Switzerland, I turn to you.

Two years ago I emigrated to the West, since it was no longer in my power to bear the extreme and hostile attitude of Party, Soviet and Sport leaders, since I no longer had the possibility to continue my creative activity in the Soviet Union.

My family remained in the Soviet Union, my wife and son. Inspite of the fact that they are loyal Soviet citizens they submitted a request in July, 1977 to emigrate from the Soviet Union. They did this, impelled by their love for a husband and a father. November, 1977 this request was refused. In private conversation Soviet police chiefs left no doubt open that the members of my family are hostages, human beings who have been chosen to suffer penance for my escape.

About one year has passed since their request for emigration. The situation of my family is now catastrophic. They have been robbed of the means of their existence and of the possibility of working or studying. The authorities confront them with suspicion and hatred, ordinary people avoid all contact with them. For my family there has now been a severe dimunition of all the rights guaranteed by the Constitution — but there has been no reduction in their duties! My son, who already a year ago declared his intention of leaving his homeland, has nevertheless been obstinately called up for military service.

You, Marshall of the Soviet Union, praise the heroism of a Muhammed Ali, who refused to fight in Vietnam. My son also does not want to fight. He does not want to be a soldier of the state which has unscrupulously degraded his father.

Is it not curious, my dear Chairman of the Supreme Soviet, that the guilty go free while it is those who are without protection who are punished, punished for their own incapacity to work, for the appearance of unhealthy sporting relations, and finally for the professional incompetence of the Soviet leaders. The practice of punishing political hostages has, unfortunately, been common throughout the entire world, but how, my dear President, does that suit the complexion of one of the regimes which significantly helps to determine world political fashions?!

In these days a Match is beginning in the Philippines for the World Chess Championship between myself and the Soviet Grandmaster and World Champion Anatoly Karpov.

Soviet leaders have declared more than once that sport must be separated from politics. It is self-evident that those states should also adhere to this principle who will participate in the World Sport Olympiad destined for Moscow in 1980.

I appeal to your political common sense, my dear General Secretary: In order to ensure that this match for the World Chess Championship should take place under normal conditions, without political complications, I beg you to allow my family to depart from the Soviet Union.

I appeal to you to demonstrate the goodwill necessary for the fulfillment of the conditions of the Helsinki International Agreement, which prescribes the reunification of divided families.

I invoke your mercy, Mr. Chairman; I beg you to show compassion for two citizens of the USSR, whose life, by decree of fate, is no longer bound to the life of Soviet society. Permit them to leave the Soviet Union.

1-7-1978   Chess Grandmaster
cc: Soviet Ambassador in Manila   Viktor Korchnoi

We protest in the strongest possible terms to the tactics of blackmail and intimidation used by the Soviet delegation in negotiations over the question of the Swiss flag. By threatening to walk out of the match the Soviets placed their hosts in an impossible situation. We shall not lower ourselves to the reciprocal use of such tactics, but ask the Filipino people not again to allow the legitimate rights of an individual to be crushed on their own soil by the weight of Soviet power.

We also ask the Soviet delegation to make public one shred of documentary evidence, either in the rules of F.I.D.E. or in the independent report submitted from the University of Heidelberg, denying Viktor Korchnoi the right to play under the Swiss flag. We are bound by the rules of F.I.D.E. to accept the decision of the jury, but challenge any independent body not operating under duress to reach the same conclusion on the basis of the same evidence.

V. KORCHNOI
P. LEEUWERIK

To the chief arbiter
Herr Lothar Schmid
Thursday July 20 1978

Dear Herr Schmid,

It was observed during the second game today that at one point a yoghourt was passed to Mr Karpov from the Soviet delegation via one of the arbiters. According to the FIDE rules for the World Championship section 4.54 "an arbiter may make and receive emergency calls at the special phone in his dressing room. There shall be no other communication into or out of the restricted area." (Restricted Area is defined in Section 4.5).

Reception of Yoghourt or alternative sustenance is evidently not countenanced by this clause, and we protest most strongly against this serious infringement of the FIDE regulations. It is clear that a cunningly arranged distribution of edible items to one player during the game, emanating from one delegation or the other, could convey a kind of code message. Thus a yoghourt after move 20 could signify "we instruct you to offer a draw"; or a sliced mango could mean "we order you to decline a draw". A dish of marinated quails' eggs could mean "play Ng4 at once" and so on. The possibilities are limitless.

The player should take all his requirements onto the stage with him at the start of the game, and no extraneous food or extra equipment should be delivered during the game. We protest against this action by the Soviet delegation during game two and request the chief arbiter to suppress all further infringements of this nature.

Yours sincerely
P. Leeuwerik
Head of Korchnoi Delegation

PINES HOTEL
AUGUST 3rd 1978

Dear Florencio,

I would like to clarify the position of our delegation on the matter of the so called Dr Zukhar, which is causing difficulty at the present stage of the world championship. Many observers (including such an impeccable source as Harry Golombek) have remarked on the apparently suspicious behaviour of Dr Zukhar during recent games. Notice has been taken of his habit of riveting his gaze onto Korchnoi as if trying to hypnotise him or otherwise influence him into playing weak moves.

It would seem that Dr Zukhar's ability at chess is severely limited yet, paradoxically, he maintains his position as close as possible to the stage for the whole five hours of every game without even rising to answer simple calls of nature — a remarkable feat which argues more than humble devotion to the noble game of chess.

Anyone involved in a creative activity, such as writing, painting, or playing chess, knows how disturbing it can be to have a hostile person staring at them while they are in the act of creation. Mr Korchnoi feels deeply disturbed by the proximity of Dr Zukhar in the auditorium and we would suggest, in the interests of fair play and of the further peaceable course of the match, that Dr Zukhar should recognise Korchnoi's complaint and voluntarily remove himself to a more distant part of the spectator area. Surely this compliance would represent normal civilized behaviour on the part of any man who appreciated that his presence was causing distress to one of the participants in the world championship.

We would naturally prefer to settle the whole matter in a friendly way without recourse to official protests. If the Soviet delegation is here simply to play chess (as they have so often claimed) then they can raise no objection to accepting their compatriot Dr Zukhar amongst their own ranks at the back of the auditorium. If, on the other hand, the Soviet delegation refuses this reasonable step it will be a sign of their bad faith and we will have to resort to official remedies. Of course, we hope to solve all problems by friendly agreement between the contending parties.

Since the Soviet delegation disowns Dr Zukhar as a member and insists on regarding him simply as a member of the public then you, Florencio, as chief organiser of the match, have total jurisdiction to direct the movements of Dr Zukhar within the auditorium in the best interests of the match. If Dr Zukhar is, indeed, not a member of the Soviet delegation then that delegation has no right to dispute your placing of Dr Zukhar within the auditorium. We would prefer that Dr Zukhar should be seated along with the bona-fide members of the USSR delegation, at a proper distance from the stage, but if this step is resisted we request the total exclusion of Dr Zukhar from the entire spectating area for the duration of the match.

Raymond Keene, Chief Second of Viktor Korchnoi

August 5, 1978

ATTN: PROF. LIM KOK ANN
Chairman of the Match Jury
World Chess Championship

MR. LOTHAR SCHMID
Chief Arbiter of the Match

MR. FLORENCIO CAMPOMANES
Organizer of the Match

Dear Sirs:

In connection with the letter of the Challenger's Second, Mr. R. Keene on 3 of August, 1978, which may be considered as a formal protest against the presence of Dr. Vladimir Zoukhar in the auditorium, who allegedly negatively influences Mr. Korchnoi, I consider it necessary to bring to your notice the following:

Doctor of Medicine Sciences, Professor Vladimir Zoukhar has arrived to the Republic of the Philippines as a member of the Soviet Delegation, but, as distinct from World Champion personal physician Professor Mikhail Guershanovitch, is not an official person foreseen by the regulations of the match.

Professor Zoukhar is an expert in problems of psychology and neurology with a many-years experience and impecable professional reputation. For the past several years, he has been consulting World Champion within the limits of his competence.

In modern sport, including chess, the problems of psychology are of recognized scientific significance and not a few sportsmen and teams make use of psychologists' services and advices in the course of the preparation period as well as during a competition.

Incidentally, in Mr. Korchnoi's book, published in Holland in 1977 and translated thereafter into other languages, the author says that in 1974 during the final candidates' match, he resorted to the services of some psychologist of Leningrad.

Being present at the Match in Baguio, Dr. V. Zoukhar attentively follows the general psycholigal condition of the World Champion including the course of a game and simultaneously which is quite natural, may watch, which is not prohibited by the regulations, the conduct of the rival.

Being seated in the auditorium, Dr. V. Zoukhar infringes upon none of the requirements concerning spectators of the section 7.4 of the regulations. The fact, that sometimes during the whole period of a game, he would not leave his seat, not even to answer simple calls of nature (to which Mr. R. Keene pays particular attention in his letter) cannot be regarded as criminal behaviour.

On the contrary, Dr. Zoukhar makes less noise or disturbance than those who repeatedly enter or leave the auditorium.

In his letter, Mr. Keene points out that the very presence of Dr. Zoukhar in the auditorium, his riveting gazes at Mr. Korchnoi disturb the latter. Mr. Keene also hints to Dr. Zoukhar's abilities of hypnotic influence.

These accusations are absolutely unproven both from scientifical and factual points of view. By the way, it would be appropriate to recollect, that similar groundless suspicions and accusations Mr. Korchnoi put forward earlier, in the matches, for instance with M. Tal (1968), A. Karpov (1974) B. Spassky (1977-1978).

Such complaints of the supernatural factors' influence in the course of the chess struggle, may be explained by either Mr. Korchnoi's un-healthy inclination to exageration or the desire to purposely complicate and sharpen the atmosphere around the so important sport competition.

In connection with this, we feel ourselves obliged to remind of the fact that many matches with Mr. Korchnoi's participation were accom-panied by scandalous situations. For instance, 1968 matches with Mr. Reschevsky and M. Tal, 1974 matches with Mr. E. Meking, T. Petrosian, A. Karpov, 1977-1978 match with B. Spassky.

Basing on the above-mentioned, we regard the accusations and sus-picions advanced against Professor Zoukhar as well as requirement to mark out his location (as distinct from other spectators) not speaking of the exclusion from the Convention Center as being groundless and unseemly.

In conclusion, I must note that the behaviour of certain official members of the challenger's delegation in the auditorium is not immacu-late and sometimes evoked discontent on the part of A. Karpov. However, World Champion, manifesting his self control did not wish to resort to police methods to have some persons ejected or replaced.

With the "hypnosis" issue being widely commented on in mass media and thus having replaced the "youghourt question", we would like to clarify our position as stated in this letter in public.

Respectfully yours,

SOVIET CHESS FEDERATION

VICTOR BATURINSKY
Vice-President

PUBLIC STATEMENT BY VIKTOR KORCHNOI
8th of August 1978

Viktor Korchnoi has requested me as his official representative, to inform the press of the following:

Mr. Karpov has made it known through his Press spokesman, Mr. Roshal, that Viktor Korchnoi has made some aspersions against him and his colleagues which has made it impossible for him to shake hands with Viktor Korchnoi in the future.

Mr. Karpov now departs from a point to which he himself agreed at the beginning of the match. For the rest, he has only agreed to this point out of deference to the Philippine People and in order to lend this strange match some elegance on the stage.

When Viktor Korchnoi chose the Philippines as the location of the match, he had in mind above all that this young and developing Republic was entirely independent from outside politics. He was convinced that the influence of Soviet politics was less here than in any European country. Viktor Korchnoi is still convinced of this and renders his thanks to the host country for its friendly hospitality and for the security and protection it has afforded him.

Viktor Korchnoi regrets to find that even in this beautiful and independent country the characteristic Soviet political maneuvering in chess, of which Robert Fischer has already been a victim, has produced on occasion substantial results.

Viktor Korchnoi would be glad if Mr. Campomanes, the organizer of the match, would follow the precept of President Marcos and not allow himself to be affected by the intimidation and blackmail of the Soviet delegation so that Mr. Campomanes may fulfill his official duties in honourable fashion.

Mr. Karpov is surrounded by many accomplished aides who are attempting to persuade the world that he is solely and purely a chess player whereas Viktor Korchnoi, bluntly speaking, is uniquely engaged in playing politics.

Can it be that Mr. Karpov really believes that the efforts of Viktor Korchnoi for the last two years to get his family out of the Soviet Union are only a pretense? Does Mr. Karpov think that in discarding the Soviet flag Viktor Korchnoi has also rejected the right to have any other flags in the world?

Viktor Korchnoi realizes that Mr. Karpov learnt in school that his country was the biggest in the world but Viktor Korchnoi hopes that the intellectual niveau of Mr. Karpov permits him to look around and perceive that, all the same, there exist other countries in the world.

Does Mr. Karpov really imagine that he is acting ethically in employing the help of a mysterious Zoukhar in order to obtain the title of World Champion, yet once again, without a fight — a world Champion of a so-called Soviet world empire?

So far as the handshaking is concerned Viktor Korchnoi declares that the reason he emigrated from the Soviet Union was precisely because he wanted to be liberated from the distasteful task of clasping hands with such people as Karpov and his crew.

Viktor Korchnoi had made the decision, at the beginning of the 9th game to cut off all friendly communication with Mr. Karpov. The offer of a draw will only be made through the Chief Arbiter, Dr. Lothar Schmid.

Viktor Korchnoi has requested me to say that from now on, until the end of the match, he will be animated by a special feeling when playing the games — he will hear, resounding in the pockets of his adversary, the clank of the chains that fetter his family in the prison camp that is the Soviet Union.

Perhaps the key of these fetters is to be found in the pockets of the innocent and honourable learned gentleman Mr. Zoukhar or of Mr. Viktor Davidowitsch Baturinsky who were professional jailers and still are such and no doubt always be.

Viktor Korchnoi would be very glad if all the journalists, in those countries where free speech is allowed, would inform their readers of this decision.

CHESS MATCH IN THE PHILIPPINES
IS NOT A TRAINING GROUND
FOR COLD WAR

Statement of the Soviet Chess Delegation at the World Chess Championship Match.

On August 8, 1978, Mrs. Leeuwerik who calls herself the head of "Swiss Chess Delegation" (no chess player of which by the way, is a citizen of Switzerland) in behalf of Mr. Korchnoi issued an official public statement.

This unprecedented document in the history of World Chess is from beginning to the end replete with crude personal insults and provocative political insinuations.

It continues and extends the tactics launched by the Challenger's group at the press conference held in Manila on July 4, 1978, when an attempt was made to insult and slander World Champion, Anatoly Karpov, some other famous grandmasters and chess representatives.

As far as the World Champion and all the persons who have arrived to the Match from the Soviet Union are concerned, none of them during their stay in the Philippines, neither orally nor in press, has allowed any insult or tactless remark in respect to the members of the Challenger's delegation or issued any political statement.

All disputes and discussions that had taken place before the beginning of the match and have been in the course of the games, including the question of the right to use national flag, all of them had sport and technical nature and dealt with the interpretations of certain points of the Regulations of the Match.

The fact, that so far the Jury of Appeals considered and decided all the problems not in favor of the Challenger, easily can be explained. His requirements and protests have been unfounded and sometimes, just ridiculous.

Members of the Jury have repeatedly been accused by the Challenger and Mrs. Leeuwerik of acting unobjectively and not being neutral. The question is that the decisions have been made by world known and respected chess leaders, FIDE Bureau and Central Committee member, Mr. E. Edmonson (USA), 10th Zone President and FIDE Central Committee member, Professor Lim Kok Ann (Singapore) FIDE Qualification Committee member, Mr. A. Malchev (Bulgaria). The Challenger did not get embarrassed to name members of the Jury "children" for their having not agreed to his claims.

Talking about this, Mr. Korchnoi's unceremoniousness and ill-bredness are well-known. Thus, in 1974, he publicly insulted the Final candidates' Match Chief Arbiter, Count Alberico O'Kelly (Belgium).

World Ex-Champion, Mikhail Tal is a popular and respected figure all the world over for his outstanding talent and sporting gentleman-ness and Mr. Korchnoi dared to name him a slanderer.

In the letter of Aug. 6, 1978, addressed to the Match Jury, he called Professor, Doctor of Medicine Sciences, V. Zoukhar "hooligan pseudo-scholar", although, in the book published in Holland in 1978 he referred to him as one of the prominent scientists.

In the statement of August 8, 1978, it is asserted that FIDE Vice President, Mr. Florencio Campomanes, allegedly fulfills his duties as the Match Organizer in an unhonourable fashion, and the authors edify him of proper behaviour.

World Champion's refusal to shake hands with his rival beginning with the 8th game, appeared to be the immediate pretext that was chosen for the statement of August 8.

In connection with this, one should be reminded of the fact that the request of shaking hands before each game, stemmed from the Challenger and was stated in his telegram to FIDE President on March 3, 1978. This prudence accounted for the fact that some of Mr. Korchnoi's rivals in previous competitions refused to shake hands with him.

Exclusively out of respect for the organizers and audience, World Champion, Anatoly Karpov agreed, however, to the traditional hand-shake procedure.

Now, in the light of the statement where it is pointed out that Mr. Korchnoi had defected from the USSR "to be liberated from distasteful task of clasping hands with such people as Karpov and his crew" especially obvious seems to have been the rightfulness of the World Champion's rejection to shake hands with Mr. Korchnoi.

Now, it is appropriate to mark here that the Challenger's second, grandmaster, Mr. R. Keene has lost the traits characterizing the English gentleman, apparently as a result of contacts with the kind of people Mrs. Leeuwerik and Mr. Korchnoi are, and allowed uncrupulous, insult-ing retort, which to our regret, was quoted in the Press.

Analizing the statement of August 8, 1978, in the agregate with other actions of the Challenger's side, one should come to the conclusion that its principal "spring" is not so much Mr. Korchnoi himself as the above-mentioned Mrs. Leeuwerik.

This woman, who never had anything to do with chess and the inter-national chess movement, who openly declares of her spiteful hatred to the USSR, is trying to convert the distinguished sporting competition, that the World Chess Championship Match is, into the training ground of the Cold War and impede the consolidation of friendship and cultural cooperation, to which admittedly serve chess, between countries.

USSR CHESS DELEGATION
Republic of the Philippines
Baguio City
August 10, 1978